SAUL KRIPKE

Continuum Contemporary American Thinkers:

John Searle, Joshua Rust

SAUL KRIPKE

ARIF AHMED

continuum

Continuum International Publishing Group
The Tower Building   80 Maiden Lane
11 York Road   Suite 704
London SE1 7NX   New York
     NY 10038
www.continuumbboks.com

British Library Cataloguing-in-Publication Data
A catalogue record for this book is available from the British Library.

ISBN-10: HB: 0–8264–9261–4
PB: 0–8264–9262–2
ISBN-13: HB: 978–0–8264–9261–6
PB: 978–0–8264–9262–3

Library of Congress Cataloging-in-Publication Data
A catalog record for this book is available from the Library of Congress.

Typeset by YHT Ltd, London
Printed and bound in Great Britain by Cormwell Press Ltd, Trowbridge,
Wiltshire

CONTENTS

ABBREVIATIONS

Those works of Kripke cited in the text and notes are abbreviated as follows:

IN: 'Identity and necessity', in M. Munitz (ed.), *Identity and Individuation*, 135–64. New York: New York University Press, 1971. Reprinted in A. W. Moore (ed.), *Meaning and Reference*. Oxford: Oxford University Press, 1993.

NN: 'Naming and necessity', in D. Davidson and G. Harman (eds), *Semantics of Natural Language*, 253–355. Dordrecht: D. Reidel, 1972.

NN2: *Naming and Necessity*. Cambridge, Mass.: Harvard University Press, 1980.

W: *Wittgenstein on Rules and Private Language*. Oxford: Blackwell, 1982.

PREFACE

I wrote this book between June and October 2006 during sabbatical leave from lecturing and teaching duties. I am grateful to the Faculty of Philosophy at Cambridge University and also to Girton College, Cambridge for granting me leave during this period. I am grateful to the Cambridge University Centre for Research in the Arts, Social Sciences and Humanities (CRASSH) for providing space in which to complete the book. I am grateful to Messrs A. Stewart-Wallace and T. Goldschmidt for helping to prepare the index. And I am grateful to Professor David Braddon-Mitchell of Sydney University for helpful discussions regarding the material in Chapter 2.

Professor Kusch's new book on Kripke's interpretation of Wittgenstein is an important and ground-breaking addition to the literature. I regret that I only had a chance to see it two weeks before I finished the present study. So I have not here given it the careful attention that it certainly deserves. But I do discuss one of Kusch's arguments in a footnote to Chapter 5, and I am very grateful to him for helpful comments on it.

I wish to thank Blackwell Publishers (UK) and Harvard University Press (US) for permission to quote from *Naming and Necessity*, and Blackwell Publishers for permission to quote from *Wittgenstein on Rules and Private Language*.

During the writing of this book the best things in my life were Isla and Frisbee (who also taught me a great deal about rule-following). So I dedicate it to them.

1

INTRODUCTION

My aim in the following is to describe and assess the main arguments in Kripke's two most important works: *Naming and Necessity* and *Wittgenstein on Rules and Private Language*. Limitations of space have prevented me from discussing everything that Kripke does. I have chosen to focus on material that is probably common to most undergraduate courses in Western philosophy. This is as follows: Kripke's rejection of the description theory (Chapter 2), essence and materialism (Chapter 3), the sceptical paradox (Chapter 4) and the argument against private language (Chapter 5). Certainly this covers most of what is taught about Kripke in the undergraduate courses most familiar to me, i.e. Part IB Logic, Part II Metaphysics and Part II Philosophical Logic in the Cambridge Tripos. Probably the two most important omissions are Kripke's outline in NN of a causal theory of reference and the postscript to W on other minds.

I am also aware that even what I *have* discussed deserves lengthier consideration. The reader should therefore take my criticisms of Kripke with an appropriate pinch of salt: no doubt he can be defended from most of them. But my aim was never to refute Kripke's views: only to present objections to them. That approach derives from my conviction that the best way to understand a position is to disagree with it. If the text drives the reader back to Kripke's own work in order to see what more might be said then it will have served its purpose.

I have tried my best throughout to follow Kripke's own admirable practice of not resorting to formal symbolism when plain English will do.

Saul Kripke was born in New York in 1940 and was appointed to the Harvard Society of Fellows in 1963. In 1968 he was appointed Associate Professor of Philosophy at Rockefeller University and in 1977 became McCosh Professor of Philosophy at Princeton. He is currently (2006) Distinguished Professor of Philosophy at the City University of New York Graduate Centre. In addition to the works considered here he has made a number of notable contributions to philosophical logic. But *Naming and Necessity* and *Wittgenstein on Rules and Private Language* are certainly his most important, influential, and accessible works, and I confine my attention to these.

Kripke's early work is best understood in the context of two important features of the philosophical scene at the time. The first was that the discipline of metaphysics – the study of such ultimate features of reality as necessity, time and causation – was in some disrepute amongst philosophers. There was pressure from two different directions towards the view that it could not be both an autonomous and a substantive subject. Wittgenstein had argued – early and late – that philosophy in general, and metaphysics in particular, was autonomous but not substantive. The true method in philosophy was to say nothing except what can meaningfully be said – propositions of natural science – and 'whenever someone else wanted to say something metaphysical, to demonstrate to him that he had failed to give a meaning to certain signs in his propositions' (1963:6.53). And Quine had argued (1951) that philosophy was substantive but not autonomous: its methods were continuous with those of natural science and its conclusions as empirically vulnerable as the latter.

The second feature of the philosophical scene was the then prevalent view that linguistic meaning is somehow mediated by something in the mind of the speaker. This thought goes back at least as far as Locke (1979, Book III), for whom the primary meaning of a term is an idea or image in the speaker's mind: and it is only *via* these ideas that a speaker's words manage to refer to or describe objects in the external world at all. The Lockean picture had certainly been modified by the twentieth century: under the influence of Frege (1956, 1960) it was now believed that your attaching a meaning to a word was not primarily a matter of your associating it with a quasi-sensory state but rather a matter of your associating it with an abstract object or sense (see 2.1.3(ii) and 4.2.7 below). But what persisted was the view that the extra-cranial reference of a word was mediated by or at any rate somehow involved its mental association with something ('sense') that itself determines the reference.

Naming and Necessity challenged both of these received views. With regard to the first: Kripke argues in NN (and also in IN) that we can through philosophical reflection alone reach substantive metaphysical conclusions concerning the intrinsic nature of things – what you might call their essence. We can for instance see that it is part of Queen Elizabeth's essence that she had her actual parents (3.1.2 below) and that if heat is molecular motion then it is essential to heat that that is what it is (3.2.4 below). Most spectacularly, we can see through reflection alone that mental states cannot be identical to physical ones (3.4 below). The faculty that delivers these wonderful results is called intuition and we shall have a good deal to say about its operation throughout Chapters 2 and 3.

With regard to the second view: Kripke gave three arguments against the Fregean position that a name (like 'London') achieves reference to objects (like London) via its user's association of it with something (a sense) that specifies its reference. These arguments are widely regarded as having discredited the Fregean doctrine. We shall consider them in detail in Chapter 2.

It is not really necessary to say very much about the context of the later work, *Wittgenstein on Rules and Private Language*. Partly this is because Kripke is not attacking some theory that had especially wide currency at the time of writing but rather a view of meaning that has always come quite naturally to everyone, i.e. that there is such a thing. And partly it is because the work is written at the level of an elementary exposition, to be used in introductory classes on Wittgenstein (W viii). It is perhaps worth mentioning that the ideas presented in W had been in the air for some time before its publication: Wright's interpretation of Wittgenstein (1980) is quite similar to Kripke's, and Fogelin's (the first edition of his 1987) is remarkably so. And I argue briefly at 4.1.3 that my interpretation of the central argument of W Chapter 2 locates it in a tradition that includes Schopenhauer and Berkeley as well as Wittgenstein himself.

But the best way to approach W is not to worry about these anticipations of it. The best way to approach it is to read the book up to p. 15. At this point the basic problem should be clear. The reader should then try to think up his own response to the problem. He should then read the rest of W Chapter 2 and see whether

Kripke has a cogent argument against this response. Then read on to the end of the book. I am confident that nobody who follows this course will complete the book without feeling that his most basic preconceptions of meaning have been profoundly disturbed: and this is a mark of its quality.

2

NAMES

The first two lectures of *Naming and Necessity* present three arguments against a specific thesis. In this chapter I describe the thesis and its motivation, and then describe and assess Kripke's arguments against it.

2.1 THE FREGE-RUSSELL THESIS

Kripke names his target the 'Frege-Russell Thesis' (henceforth FRT) and describes it as follows:

> Really a proper name, properly used, [is] simply a definite description abbreviated or disguised. Frege specifically said that such a description gave the sense of the name. (NN:255/NN2:27)

Kripke thinks that FRT is false: but before saying why, we should say a little more about what it is.

2.1.1 What it is

To see what it amounts to we must explain 'proper name', 'definite description', 'abbreviation' and 'sense'.

(i) 'Proper name' means a name for some object, e.g. a city, a man, a star or a number (NN:254/NN2:24). Proper names purport to have no explicitly descriptive element. Hence 'Britain' qualifies as the name of a country whereas 'The United Kingdom' arguably doesn't (if it purports to *describe* rather than simply to *specify* a country) and 'The country whose capital is London' certainly doesn't.

(ii) 'Definite description' means a phrase that purports to specify an object by describing it as the unique possessor of some property. In English this is normally done by means of the definite article. Thus 'The King of France in 1789' is a definite description since it purports to specify one man. And in fact there is just one man satisfying it, i.e. Louis XVI. If the property F belongs to more or less than one thing then 'The F' doesn't specify any thing at all. But it still purports to do so: it therefore counts none the less as a definite description. 'The king of France in 1830' and 'The King of France in 1905' are both definite descriptions even though there was more than one French king in 1830 and fewer in 1905. If F belongs to no thing then the definite description 'The F' is called *empty*.

(iii) 'Abbreviation' normally carries two connotations that are irrelevant here and one that is relevant. If expression X is said to 'abbreviate' expression Y then it normally follows (a) that X takes less time or space to say or write than Y; (b) that X was explicitly introduced into the language as a substitute for Y; (c) that X means the same as Y. Thus each of (a)-(c) follows from the fact that 'A.A.' abbreviates 'Alcoholics Anonymous'. But 'abbreviation' in the context of FRT implies neither (a) nor (b). In this slightly technical usage it would be true to say that 'Michelangelo Buonarotti' abbreviates 'The sculptor of *David*' even though the name is neither shorter than nor introduced explicitly to replace the description. All that remains is the bare assertion of synonymy: each name means the same as some definite description.

(iv) A proper grasp of the notion of sense is so closely tied up with the reason for believing in it that its explanation must wait until we have seen what the reason is (at 2.1.3(ii)).

For the moment we can say this: FRT is the theory that a name means what some definite description means. For example: 'Napoleon Bonaparte' means what 'The Emperor of the French who was defeated at Waterloo' does. But there are actually two versions of it, as follows.

2.1.2 Pure and Impure Versions of It

A *demonstrative* is an expression that refers to some ostended item (or at any rate purports to). 'This man' is being used as a demonstrative when accompanied e.g. by a pointing gesture at some visible man. An *indexical* is an expression whose reference depends on the temporal or spatial location of the speaker, or on some other circumstance of the speaker that may vary from one occasion to another. A *pure* definite description is one that contains no names, demonstratives or indexicals. All other definite descriptions are called *impure*. For example, 'The smallest round thing' is a pure definite description; and both 'The father of that man' and 'The present King of France' are impure definite descriptions (Hughes 2004: 6–7).

A pure definite description specifies something in purely qualitative terms. It could be understood by someone who had no idea of where or when or in what surroundings it was uttered, and who didn't yet know the name of *anything*, so long as he understood the qualities that it mentioned.

The *pure* version of FRT (henceforth PV) says that every name means what some *pure* definite description does. The impure version of FRT (henceforth IV) says that each name means the same as some definite description, pure or impure.

Imagine that God, who exists at no place or time, created the universe and all its history simply by stipulating what collections of properties were instantiated, without speaking of 'here' or 'now' or using any names. Thus he might stipulate e.g. that a man fitting a certain description exists who eats an apple and thereby incurs punishment etc. (creating but not naming Adam) and that thousands of years later a city fitting such and such description with a domed cathedral should exist (creating but not naming London). The pure version of FRT – what I am calling PV – then amounts to this. If after this act of creation God had then annexed its name to each of the individuals created by his purely descriptive decree, then the names could have meant what they actually do (cf. Wittgenstein 1963: 5.526).

The less ambitious theory IV makes no such claim. It only says that the meaning of a name is that of some pure *or* impure description. The proponent of IV can say that 'Rome' means the same as 'The city founded by Romulus' without having to say that the latter description must itself have some purely qualitative analysis.

It sometimes seems that Kripke's target is the pure and not the impure version of FRT. For example, he says at one point:

> It seems to be wrong to think that we give ourselves some properties which somehow qualitatively uniquely pick out an object and determine our reference in that manner. (NN:300/NN2:93–4)

But if all Kripke's arguments show is the falsity of PV then they are not very interesting. We shall see in a moment that the central arguments for FRT support IV, not PV. Moreover PV is quite implausible for much more straightforward reasons than Kripke's.[1] Fortunately it turns out that Kripke's own arguments are equally effective against both IV and PV. From now on IV will be the main focus of interest.

2.1.3 Reasons for Believing It
Why think FRT is true? Kripke mentions three reasons: I will discuss these and a couple of others.

(i) The first argument (NN:256/NN2:28) is that unless names abbreviate definite descriptions it is hard to see how they can refer at all. 'Napoleon' refers to a particular man – but how? It is just a collection of letters written in the twenty-first century: what can that have to do with a man who lived in the nineteenth? What makes it to do with him rather than any other particular man? FRT implies a straightforward answer: 'Napoleon' abbreviates a description satisfied by that man and no other. The fact that FRT can solve this problem so simply is a reason to believe it.

Note that the argument does not support the pure version of FRT but the impure one. The problem was how a name can refer to a thing. The answer is that it refers because the thing satisfies the description associated with the name. This answer does not and need not require the associated description to be pure. Even if the description is impure – e.g. if it involves an indexical – we still have some sort of explanation of how names refer. To complete the explanation we should need an account of how the impure – e.g. the indexical – part of the description refers. But nothing in this argument for FRT rules out any such account.

(ii) The second argument (NN:256–7/NN2:28) has two parts. The first part shows that names that refer to the same thing can have different meanings. The second shows that in this case the names will have the meanings of definite descriptions. Our example is the true sentence 'Eric Blair is George Orwell'. (He was christened Eric Blair but took the pen-name George Orwell.)

Suppose you know your next-door neighbour to be Eric Blair and also that George Orwell is the author of *Animal Farm*. But you are unaware that these are the same person. Then 'Eric Blair is George Orwell' expresses a truth that you'd find surprising. It must therefore have different informational content from 'Eric Blair is Eric Blair', which you already knew. What then *is* its informational content? Plausibly this: that your next-door neighbour is the author of *Animal Farm*.

We can express the first part of this argument slightly more formally. This will help us to define the notion of *sense* that Kripke had in mind when he said that for Frege 'the sense of a name is a definite description'. The argument proceeds by supposing that 'Eric Blair' means the same as 'George Orwell' and deriving an obvious falsehood:

(1) 'Eric Blair' means the same as 'George Orwell' (Supposition)
(2) If two names mean the same then you can substitute one for the other in a sentence without changing the meaning of the sentence (Premise)
(3) If two sentences mean the same then they convey the same information (Premise)
(4) 'Eric Blair is Eric Blair' means the same as 'Eric Blair is George Orwell' (from 1, 2)
(5) 'Eric Blair is George Orwell' conveys the same information as 'Eric Blair is Eric Blair' (from 3, 4)

Now plainly (5) is false. But it follows from the premises (1), (2) and (3) by the reasoning just stated. Given the initial plausibility of (2) and (3) it follows that (1) is false: 'Eric Blair' and 'George Orwell' refer to the same thing but have different meanings. So there must be some component to the meaning of a name other than its reference wherein 'Eric Blair' and 'George Orwell' differ.

It is this additional component of meaning that we call *sense*. What kind of thing is a sense? Well, it is whatever our argument has shown to exist. Now the argument shows that the names 'Eric Blair' and 'George Orwell' make differing contributions to the informational content of sentences containing them. We may therefore think of the sense of a name as just that: the contribution it makes to the informational content of a sentence containing it. So if 'Eric Blair' and 'George Orwell' have different senses then 'Eric Blair is George Orwell' conveys different information from 'Eric Blair is Eric Blair'. This is as you would expect.

But what *is* the contribution of a particular name? It is here that definite descriptions come in. Consider the sentence 'Eric Blair wrote *Animal Farm*'. What information does it convey? For you it conveys the same as 'My next-door neighbour wrote *Animal Farm*'. This and similar examples suggest that for many names N, the information conveyed by 'N is F' is that conveyed by 'The G is F', where 'The G' is a definite description. It follows that the sense of the name N – its contribution to the informational content of sentences containing it – is that of some definite description 'The G'. (E.g. the sense of 'Eric Blair' is that of the definite description '[The man who is] my next-door neighbour'.) This is the Frege-Russell Thesis.

There are three things to note about the argument.

The first is that its second part is weak. At best it shows that *some* names have the sense of a definite description. It doesn't show that *all* names have such a sense or that any name *must* have it. Still, it does in conjunction with the first part of the argument make it plausible that *many* proper names have the sense of a definite description. And we shall see that Kripke's arguments resist this conclusion even for cases where the second part of the argument most plausibly applies. So even if the argument shows only that the sense of many proper names of English is that of a definite description, it remains the case that Kripke would resist its conclusion.

The second point is that the argument doesn't show that every (or any) name has a *single* sense for all speakers. What information a sentence conveys will vary from one speaker to another. It may be that 'Eric Blair is George Orwell' conveys to *you* the same as 'My next-door neighbour is George Orwell' and to *me* the same as 'My grandfather's best friend is George Orwell'. At best we can say that *each* person associates with a proper name some definite description that specifies the name's sense. Frege himself certainly recognized that sense may vary from one person to another (Frege 1960:58n). And Kripke understood FRT in this way too (NN:280/NN2:64).

Note finally that the argument doesn't favour PV over IV. This is clear from the example: so far as the argument is concerned, the sense associated by any speaker with 'Eric Blair' may be that of the impure description '*My* next-door neighbour'.

(iii) The third argument (NN:257/NN2:29) is based upon the fact that one can meaningfully use a proper name to ask whether something exists at all. And the meaningfulness of the question seems not to vary between cases where the answer is yes and cases where it is no. One can ask 'Does Santa Claus exist?' just as sensibly as one can ask 'Did Aristotle exist?' But what *is* the meaning of the first question? It can hardly be that there is some thing (Santa Claus) whose existence you are querying: there isn't. The more natural interpretation of the question is this: it queries the satisfaction of certain properties: in the first case it is a question about whether there is someone who gives presents to all children on Xmas day and in the second it is a question about whether (say) there is some one author of such and such books. But this interpretation seems to compel us to identify the meaning of 'Santa Claus' with that of a definite description ('The man who gives presents ...') – and the same is true of 'Aristotle'.

Note again that the argument establishes no more than IV. There is no requirement that the description substituted for 'Santa Claus' mention no names at all: all that is required is that the ultimate analysis mentions no names or other terms referring to items whose existence under that name cannot sensibly be questioned. There may indeed be such items and terms (one example might be 'I'). Whether or not there are is a further question not settled by this argument.

As well as the three arguments that Kripke mentions, I will mention two others. These arguments present FRT as arising from certain broad philosophical conceptions of man and his place in nature. I am not mentioning them in order to endorse them but only to illustrate how the significance of FRT goes beyond the philosophy of language: it raises issues in metaphysics and epistemology too.

(iv) One argument for FRT comes from dualism. This is the view that there are two kinds of thing in the universe – mind and matter, where by 'mind' is meant not just one's sensations but also one's thoughts. According to dualism the content of your thought is a radically different sort of thing from the material world around you. One might describe this gulf in terms of a radical sort of independence: the thought you have would have been the very same thought regardless of the contents or even the existence of the material world (McDowell 1977:125–6). So if you are having the thought, e.g. that Aristotle is a great philosopher, then that very thought might have existed even if nothing material had existed – and in particular if Aristotle had not existed. But then it ought to be possible to describe this thought about Aristotle in some way that makes no mention of him. (Compare: the fact that some things would be red even if there were no tomatoes implies that it must be possible to describe redness in some way other than as the colour of tomatoes.) But then FRT – understood now as being about the thoughts expressed by our words – points to just such an analysis. It implies that the very thought *that Aristotle was a great philosopher* can be described in terms that do not mention Aristotle at all, e.g. as the thought *that the author of these books was a great philosopher*.[2] The only names that do not fall under the scope of this argument will be names either of mental entities themselves or of objects whose very existence is necessary.

There is much to contest in this argument. It is e.g. hardly clear that if the existence of a thought about Aristotle is independent of Aristotle then that thought really must be describable in terms that do not mention him. As I said, I am not mentioning this line of thought in order to endorse it but only to illustrate the cohesion between a metaphysical position (dualism) and a semantic one (FRT). Note also that even if valid, this argument need not push us into accepting the *pure* version of FRT (PV). If the dualist who takes this line thinks that the indexical 'I' refers to an immaterial entity (his self or soul) then he will grant that that indexical may appear somewhere in the analysis of a proper name N and can therefore allow that any definite description that gives the meaning of N is itself impure.

(v) The final argument for FRT is epistemological. Well-known sceptical arguments may show that I can never know that an external world exists. But I can still be certain of the *meanings* of my words. But if I can be certain in particular of the meanings of proper names, then those words must have meanings that do *not* require the existence of what they supposedly refer to, unless they refer to something of which I am certain. One way to satisfy this requirement is to analyse names in terms of definite descriptions that do *not* mention the thing that the names refer to unless that thing can itself be known with certainty. More precisely: the proper names of English grasped by a speaker will fall into two categories: those that refer to items known to the speaker; and those that do not. Then FRT will apply to the latter class of names, because it analyses them into definite descriptions that mention only things known to the speaker (e.g. qualities).

Again, I do not mean to endorse the argument: I mention it only to illustrate the possibility of some intuitive cohesion between FRT and a certain kind of scepticism. Note also that the argument doesn't require every speaker to associate a definite description with *every* name. It only shows that he associates a description with names that apparently refer to things that he cannot know. In particular a speaker may *not* need to associate a description with a name for himself, if one can (as Descartes believed and Hume denied) have certain knowledge of one's self:

> Assuming that there is such a thing as direct acquaintance with oneself, Bismarck himself might have used his name directly to designate the particular with whom he was acquainted ... Here the proper name has the direct use which it always wishes to have, as simply standing for a certain object, and not for a description of the object. (Russell 1959: 54)

Note finally that the argument as presented doesn't force the sceptic to go as far as the pure version of FRT (PV). As far as this argument is concerned a speaker may perfectly well associate proper names with definite descriptions including names for *himself*, if one can indeed have knowledge of oneself. So as far as this argument goes there is no impetus towards accepting PV: it is only an argument for IV.

So we have five arguments for FRT: (i) from the possibility of reference; (ii) from true identity statements; (iii) from meaningful queries about existence; (iv) from dualism; (v) from scepticism. None of the arguments establishes PV: they only establish IV. If Kripke's aim is to cast doubt on the position motivated by at least arguments (i)–(iii) then his arguments should be directed against IV. That is how I will interpret them.

2.1.4 A Modification

Before considering Kripke's central arguments, one straightforward objection to FRT must be got out of the way. It is highly implausible to tie the meaning of a name to any *one* definite description. As Kripke says:

> If 'Aristotle' meant *the man who taught Alexander the Great* then saying 'Aristotle was a teacher of Alexander the Great' would be

a mere tautology ... So, *being the teacher of Alexander the Great* cannot be part of the sense of the name. (NN:257–8/NN2:30)

Now plainly there are *some* names which when conjoined with an associated description yield tautologies for most speakers, e.g. 'Jack the Ripper was the person who committed these murders' (NN:291/ NN2:79–80). But equally plainly Kripke is right about most names. For any single definite description D known to be satisfied by Aristotle, the sentence 'Aristotle was D' isn't tautologous for most speakers. Hence 'Aristotle' doesn't mean the same as any such description: so FRT is false.

There is, however, a modified theory that retains the spirit of FRT (being equally well motivated by the arguments 2.1.3(i)–(v)) while abandoning its letter (NN:257/NN2:31). The modified theory is called the *cluster theory* and it says this: the meaning associated with a name by a speaker is given by a *family* of definite descriptions: its meaning is roughly 'whatever satisfies most of the descriptions in the family'. Suppose we know these three things about Aristotle – he was (a) *The greatest philosopher of Antiquity*; (b) *The Author of such and such books*; and (c) *The teacher of Alexander the Great*. Then the meaning of Aristotle will according to the cluster theory be that of 'Whoever satisfies most of (a)–(c)'. It is on this view not a tautology to say that Aristotle was the teacher of Alexander the Great, for it isn't a tautology to say that the man who satisfies *most* of (a)–(c) (i.e. two of them) in fact satisfies (c).

I said that this was only a rough characterization of the cluster theory. Stated more precisely, it requires that the members of the associated family of descriptions make differently *weighted* contributions to the meaning of the name. The notion of weight may be illustrated by considering what it would take to confirm the discovery that, contrary to what people thought, the bearer of some name N did not exist. Consider Wittgenstein's example of Moses (Wittgenstein 1967: section 79). If it were discovered e.g. that Pharaoh's daughter rescued nobody as a baby, I think we (or those people who believe this stuff) should still say that Moses *existed*, only that his infancy didn't in fact contain an incident widely supposed to have occurred in it. If on the other hand we discovered that nobody led the Israelites out of Egypt or that nobody received the Ten Commandments then the temptation to say that Moses never existed would be stronger. This shows that the descriptions *person who led the Israelites out of Egypt* and *person who received the Ten Commandments* make weightier contributions to the meaning of 'Moses' than the description *person who was rescued as an infant by Pharaoh's daughter*. At any rate they make weightier contributions to the meaning of that name in the context 'Moses did not exist'. More generally, we may say that a description D1 carries greater weigh than a description D2 with respect to a name N if for any predicate F, 'D1 was F' is better grounds for asserting 'N was F' than is 'D2 wasn't F' for denying it.

We can summarize all this by identifying the meaning of a name N not with that of 'The thing that satisfies most of these descriptions' but with that of 'the thing that satisfies a *weighted* most of these descriptions' (NN:280–1/NN2:64–5).

This brings the essential vagueness of the cluster theory into focus. How many associated descriptions – and which ones – need to be shown empty or mistaken before we can count ourselves as having discovered the non-existence of Moses as opposed to widespread error about him? The theory gives no answer. But then it doesn't need to; there seems to be *nothing* in the rules governing linguistic practice to determine the answer. The vagueness of the cluster theory seems genuinely to reflect an appropriate semantic indecision. Nothing in reality settles whether we should say 'Moses was never rescued by Pharaoh's daughter; nor did he lead the Israelites out of servitude; nor did he receive the Ten Commandments' or 'Moses never existed'. 'You can say what you like as long as you know all the facts.'

Putting aside worries over vagueness, we have the following theory. The meaning of a name for a speaker is that of an associated family of definite descriptions: the name is understood to denote whatever satisfies a weighted most of those descriptions. This theory, the cluster theory, I abbreviate as FRTC. It has two versions depending on whether or not the associated descriptions are required to be pure: I denote these PVC and IVC respectively. It is IVC that remains the most plausible and best-motivated version of the Frege-Russell Thesis. This thesis is Kripke's principal target in Lectures I and II of *Naming and Necessity*.

But it isn't always his explicit target. Some Kripkean arguments are directed explicitly against the unmodified theory FRT (or IV). The reason for this is simplicity of exposition. Some Kripkean arguments will work against both (pure and impure versions of) FRT and FRTC if they work against either. It is therefore a harmless simplification to pretend that one is arguing against FRT when one really has FRTC in one's sights. The reader should bear in mind that this is what Kripke and his critics often do (Dummett 1981a: 135–6).

2.2 THE MODAL ARGUMENT

This is Kripke's most celebrated argument against FRT. In order to grasp it, we need first to understand his terminology of metaphysical possibility, possible worlds and rigidity.

2.2.1 Metaphysical Possibility and Possible Worlds

When I say 'It might rain tomorrow or it might not' or 'such and such mathematical conjecture might be true and might be false' I am most naturally understood as expressing ignorance as to which alternative actually obtains. Similarly if I say 'It might rain tomorrow' I am probably saying that I don't know that it *won't* rain tomorrow. More generally 'It might be the case that p' usually means 'I don't know that not-p'; hence also 'it might be the case that p and it might be the case that not-p' usually means 'I don't know *whether p*'. Let us say that if a person at a time doesn't know that not-p then p is *epistemically possible* for that person at that time (so p will be epistemically possible for you at a time if you *know* that p). The words 'could' and 'possibly' mean the same. Alternatives concerning my past as well as my future can be epistemically possible for me: 'The murderer might have been Smith and it might have been Jones: but I don't know which.'

There is, however, another way of understanding 'might', 'could' and 'possibly' (NN:261–2/NN2:35–6). This is most obvious when those words are being used to justify regret or remorse. 'I might have saved him from drowning. If only I had jumped in!' expresses regret that one did *not* jump in. Clearly 'might' cannot in this context be expressing *epistemic* possibility. On that interpretation 'I might have saved him from drowning' expresses your lack of knowledge that you didn't save him. But we all *know* that you didn't: it hardly makes sense to regret what you don't know about.

The meaning of 'might' in this context is rather this: there is an alternative (or *counterfactual*) course of history where you do save him from drowning. The existence of this alternative and its status as such are unaffected by one's knowledge that the world did not take this course. We think every day about alternative ways that things might have gone while knowing all along that they were unrealized. Thoughts of this kind form the basis for regret and remorse. They are also involved in fascinating but always inconclusive exercises in counterfactual history (what would have happened if Napoleon had not invaded Russia?). Let us say that if there *is* an alternative course of history on which *p* is true, or if *p* is *actually* true, then it is *metaphysically possible* that *p*.

One can make talk about alternative possibilities more vivid by talking about 'possible worlds'. 'Possible world' is really another way to say 'alternative course of history'. Someone who says 'Napoleon might not have invaded Russia' might equally have said 'In some alternative course of history Napoleon did not invade Russia' or 'At some possible world Napoleon did not invade Russia'. It is metaphysically possible that *p* if and only if *p* is true at some possible world.

One may wish to compare how things might have been with how they in fact were. The word 'actually' is useful in this connection. It is a device for describing something as having in fact occurred or obtained. To adapt Russell's example: 'My yacht might have been bigger than it is' is ambiguous. It might mean (though this is absurd) that there is a possible world where one's yacht is bigger than it is *in that world*. Or it might mean (what isn't absurd) that one's yacht is in fact a certain size and it might have been bigger than *that*. You can indicate the latter by saying 'My yacht might have been bigger than it *actually* is.' And we will use the sign '@' to denote the actual world. The fact that if something is actual then it is metaphysically possible implies that @ is a possible world too: so in some possible world (namely @) Napoleon *does* invade Russia.

One must keep in mind the distinction between what one's words mean or refer to when they are being used (in @) to talk *about* other possible worlds and what they *would* mean if used *in* those possible worlds. It is possible that the English predicate 'flies' should mean what we actually mean by 'has a curly tail'. In a possible world where 'flies' *does* mean that, the sentence 'Pigs fly' is true because there it means that pigs have curly tails. But it is *false* to say that at that possible world pigs fly: when we use English to describe a possible world we use its words with their *actual* meaning, and at that world the actual meaning of 'flies' doesn't apply to pigs (NN:289–90/NN2:77–8).

There is plenty of controversy amongst philosophers as to whether possible worlds exist and what they are like. Some believe that there is, somewhere in the universe, a physical realm corresponding to each possibility. Others think that possible worlds exist but are not physical. But nor are they mental; on this view they are abstract objects like sets and numbers. Kripke himself seems to incline to this (NN2:17). But the arguments against FRT are independent of the issue. All we need to grasp is the relation just described between metaphysical possibility and possible worlds, whatever the latter should turn out to be.

2.2.2 Rigid and Accidental Designation

All this terminology has been leading up to the key distinction between rigid and accidental designation. This is introduced as follows:

> Let's call something [i.e. a term] a *rigid designator* if in every possible world it designates the same object, a *nonrigid* or *accidental* designator if this is not the case. Of course we don't require that the objects exist in all possible worlds. Certainly Nixon might not have existed if his parents had not gotten married, in the normal course of things ... A rigid designator of a necessary existent can be called *strongly rigid* ... For example, 'the President of the U.S. in 1970' designates a certain man, Nixon; but someone else (e.g. Humphrey) might have been the President in 1970, and Nixon might not have; so this designator is not rigid. (NN:269–70/NN2:48–9)

There are two points to make about this passage.

Firstly: when Kripke says that a rigid designator *r* designates the same object 'in' every possible world, he means that when *we* use *r* to talk *about* a possible world we are always referring to the same object. The fact that language-users in some other possible world use 'Nixon' to refer to someone other than the actual Nixon doesn't show that 'Nixon' is not a rigid designator.

Secondly (and this only makes sense when one grasps the first point): Kripke seems here to be saying that a rigid designator *r* refers to the same thing when talking about *any* possible worlds, *including* ones where the referent of *r* does not exist. So in the sentence 'If Nixon's parents had never met then Nixon would never have been born', the term 'Nixon' refers to Nixon himself rather than to nothing. There is, however, a question as to which of the following Kripke meant by 'rigid designator':

(a) A term that refers to the same thing in all possible worlds where it refers to anything at all
(b) A term that refers to the same thing in all possible worlds where that thing exists
(c) A term that refers to the same thing in all possible worlds where that thing exists and in all other worlds to nothing
(d) A term that refers to the same thing in all possible worlds

An example of type (a) that is not an example of type (b), (c) or (d) is 'The smallest factor of my favourite number'. This designates the number 1 in any world where it designates anything at all, so the term satisfies (a). But there are worlds where the number 1 exists but I do not: hence the term fails to satisfy (b)–(d). Following Hughes (2004: 20) we may call terms of type (a) *inflexible* designators. I introduce the term *mildly rigid* to characterize terms of type (b). Following Salmon (1982: 33–4) we may call terms of type (c) *persistently rigid* designators and terms of type (d) *obstinately rigid* designators. The passage just quoted suggests that what Kripke had in mind was obstinate rigidity. But another remark from around the time of NN makes clear that he actually intended *persistent* rigidity:

> All I mean is that in any possible world where the object in question *does* exist, in any situation where the object *would* exist, we use the designator in question to designate that object. In a situation where the object does not exist, then we should say that the designator has no referent and that the object in question so designated does not exist. (IN:173)

I therefore assume from now on that Kripke intends 'rigidity' to mean persistent rigidity: though we shall see that some of the other notions will serve for certain purposes.[3]

2.2.3 The Modal Argument

Kripke's modal argument is foreshadowed at NN:273/NN2:53. It is fully stated at NN:278–9/NN2:61–3 and again at NN:287–9/NN2:74–6. It runs as follows:

> The [cluster theory] would say that a name is simply *defined*, synonymously, as the cluster of descriptions. It will then be necessary, not that Moses had any particular property in this cluster, but that he had the disjunction of them. There couldn't be any counterfactual situation in which he didn't do any of those things ... Such a suggestion ... must clearly be false. Most of the things commonly attributed to Aristotle are things that Aristotle might not have done at all. (NN:278–9/NN2:61)

In order to analyse the argument we make one simplification. We shall assume that the target theory says that the meaning of 'Aristotle' is given by a *single* definite description, in this case 'The teacher of Alexander the Great'. This is harmless: if Kripke's argument works against the cluster theory then it will work against this simplified version (and conversely).

We may write the argument as follows:

(1) If 'Aristotle' means the same as 'The teacher of Alexander' then it is necessarily the case that Aristotle was the teacher of Alexander (Premise)
(2) It is not necessarily the case that Aristotle was the teacher of Alexander (Premise)
(3) If FRT is true then 'Aristotle' means the same as 'The teacher of Alexander' (Premise)
(4) 'Aristotle' does not mean the same as 'The teacher of Alexander' (from 1, 2)
(5) FRT is false (from 3, 4)

The argument is plainly valid. So its success depends entirely on the truth of its premises, which we consider separately.

2.2.4 Its First Premise

Although Kripke does state premise (1) in just this way it is strictly false for an obvious but harmless reason. After all, even if 'Aristotle' does mean the same as 'The teacher of Alexander', one might still admit that Aristotle might never have been born and hence that he might not have been the teacher of Alexander. What premise (1) should say is that if 'Aristotle' means the same as 'The teacher of Alexander' then he must have been the teacher of Alexander *provided that he existed at all*.

Kripke gives little in the way of argument for this premise although it is presupposed throughout *Naming and Necessity* (see e.g. NN:276/NN2:57). Nor is it clear that Frege and Russell themselves would have endorsed it. Frege nowhere to my knowledge discusses metaphysical necessity. And Russell denied that it makes sense to attribute necessity to propositions: and he saw the necessity of a propositional *function* (e.g. If x was Aristotle then x was the teacher of Alexander) as consisting solely in its applying truly to all *actual* things (Russell 1919:165).

What arguments are there for (1)? One argument proceeds from a generalization of the assumption (used in favour of FRT at 2.1.3(ii)) that if two names mean the same then you can substitute one for the other in a sentence without changing the meaning of that sentence. The generalization of this assumption is that if any two *expressions* mean the same then you can substitute one for the other in a sentence without changing the meaning of that sentence. The argument would then proceed as follows:

(6) If any two expressions mean the same then you can substitute one for the other in a sentence without changing the meaning of that sentence (Premise)

(7) 'Aristotle' means the same as 'The teacher of Alexander' (Supposition)

(8) 'Necessarily, Aristotle (provided he existed) was the teacher of Alexander' means the same as 'Necessarily, the teacher of Alexander (provided he existed) was the teacher of Alexander' (from 6, 7)

(9) 'Necessarily, the teacher of Alexander (provided he existed) was the teacher of Alexander' is true (Premise)

(10) 'Necessarily, Aristotle (provided he existed) was the teacher of Alexander' is true (from 8, 9)

(11) Necessarily, Aristotle (provided he existed) was the teacher of Alexander (from 10)

(1)   If 'Aristotle' means the same as 'The teacher of Alexander' then necessarily, Aristotle (provided he existed) was the teacher of Alexander (from 11, discharging 7)

This argument is valid: so does it establish premise (1)? It need not, because one might question premise (6).

Here is a counterexample (from Dummett, who uses it differently: 1981b: 568–9). Consider the expressions 'here' and 'where I am'. It is plausible that they have the same meaning for any speaker at any time. But they cannot always be interchanged without changing the meaning of sentences involving them. For example, the following two sentences have different meanings:

(e)   It is always noisy where I am
(f)   It is always noisy here

That (e) and (f) have different meanings follows from this: it suffices for (e) but not (f) that a commotion always accompanies me. What (f) requires is that I be standing at the time of utterance in a place that is perpetually noisy even when I have left it (e.g. the Niagara Falls). Hence (6) is false.

But should we not instead conclude from this example that 'here' and 'where I am' have *different* meanings? We need not. Consider the sentence:

(g)   Where I am is such that: it is always noisy *there*

Now it is plausible that (g) *does* mean the same as (f) and not the same as (e). But the difference between (e) and (g) is only one of *scope*: in (g) 'where I am' has wide scope, i.e. it specifies a place, of which the material after the colon then says that it is always noisy. Whereas in (e) 'where I am' has narrow scope, i.e. it doesn't specify a particular place but rather is governed by 'always': it specifies different places for each of the times in the scope of that quantifier. We may now maintain the intuitive thesis that 'here' and 'where I am' mean the same *subject to the convention that the latter takes wide scope in 'always'-contexts.* The addition of the convention doesn't stop 'here' from being defined in terms of 'where I am'. The convention functions as a 'stage-direction' for the elimination of 'here' in favour of 'where I am' in a particular case (Quine 1976:55).

Now the defender of FRT says the same about (6) applied to 'Aristotle' and 'The Teacher of Alexander'. He says that these two expressions *do* mean the same *subject to the convention that the definite description takes wide scope in modal contexts.* 'Aristotle' means 'The teacher of Alexander': but 'Necessarily, Aristotle was F' means 'The teacher of Alexander is such that: necessarily *he* was F'. The definite description first specifies an actual man (Aristotle) who is then said to be necessarily F (this is the analogue of (g)). Call this modified Frege-Russell Thesis 'FRTW'. FRTW retains the spirit of FRT: it is equally motivated by the arguments (i)–(v) outlined at 2.1.3.

But now the proponent of FRTW can deny Kripke's premise (1). For consider the sentences:

(h) Necessarily: Aristotle (provided he existed) was the teacher of Alexander
(i)   Necessarily: the teacher of Alexander (provided he existed) was the teacher of Alexander
(j)   The teacher of Alexander is such that: necessarily (provided he existed), he was the teacher of Alexander

Premise (6) implies that if 'Aristotle' means what 'the teacher of Alexander' does then (h) means the same as (i). But the defender of FRTW can deny this and claim on the contrary that (h) means the same as (j), not (i). For him, the synonymy of 'Aristotle' and 'the teacher of Alexander' implies not that (h) is true because (i) is true, but rather that (h) is false because (j) is false.

This argument for premise (1) therefore fails. However, Kripke does suggest another one. And considerations of scope are power-less to evade it. He writes:[4]

Consider:
(k) Aristotle was fond of dogs
A proper understanding of this statement involves an under-standing both of the (extensionally correct) conditions under which it is in fact true, *and* of the conditions under which a counterfactual course of history, resembling the actual course in some respects but not in others, would be correctly (partially) described by (k). (NN2:6)

How is this supposed to help with premise (1)? Well, what Kripke says about (k) presumably also applies to each of the following:

(l) Aristotle (provided he existed) was the teacher of Alexander
(m) The teacher of Alexander (provided he existed) was the teacher of Alexander

Sentences (l) and (m) have no room for ambiguity of scope: the proponent of FRTW is therefore just as committed as the proponent of FRT to saying that (l) and (m) have the same meaning. But if the *understanding* of sentences (l) and (m) involves a grasp of their use to describe *counterfactual* situations (other possible worlds) then presumably two sentences that mean the same must be used in the *same* way in counterfactual contexts. Hence if (m) is true of all counterfactual situations then so is (l): and this implies to premise (1).

We can put the argument like this:

(12) If 'Aristotle' means the same as 'the teacher of Alexander' then (l) means the same as (m) (Premise)
(13) If (l) means the same as (m) then: (l) is necessarily true if and only if (m) is necessarily true (Premise)
(14) (m) is necessarily true (Premise)
(15) If (l) means the same as (m) then (l) is necessarily true (from 13, 14)
(1) If 'Aristotle' means the same as 'The teacher of Alexander' then necessarily, Aristotle (provided he existed) was the teacher of Alexander (from 12, 15)

Now this argument is valid. And its premise (12) is irrefragable even for the proponent of FRTW. It contains no modal expressions at all and hence has no room for scope distinctions (NN2:11). On the other hand we may question (13) as follows.[5]

It is easy to imagine a community of language-users – perhaps some earlier stage of our own – that knows nothing of metaphysical possibility. It will of course have a conception of *epistemic* possibility but neither the language nor its speakers will display or possess any conception of how things *might* have been, in what we are calling the metaphysical sense. Now in that community no difference will be visible between sentences that in English differ only in their use to describe alternative possibilities (like (l) and (m)); there will be as good reason as can be for an interpreter of that language to affirm the synonymy of (l) with (m), or of 'Aristotle was fond of dogs' with 'The teacher of Alexander was fond of dogs'. The two members of each pair will be assented to or dissented from in just the same circumstances. To all appearances they would make the same claim about reality. In so far as it ever makes sense to say that two sentences convey the same information it will be correct to say it of *these* sentences: hence they will have the same sense.

Now what happens when we expand this language to include descriptions of metaphysical possibilities? Of course it will now be true that *some* uses of these pairs of sentences will diverge: in particular (m) but not (l) will be assertible of all counterfactual situations. But why should *this* divergence in use make a difference to the *meanings* of (l) and (m) (as asserted by (13))? What was said before can still be said: that the assent- and dissent-conditions of the two sentences are uniform; that they make the same claim about the *real* world (though different claims about fantasy-worlds); that they convey the same information. All of this is compatible with (m)'s being metaphysically necessary and (l)'s being metaphysically contingent. There seems just as much reason as before to maintain that (l) and (m) have the same meaning.

Of course the whole issue really turns on what we *mean* by 'same meaning' or 'synonymy'. What is the theoretical point of classifying pairs of sentences or expressions into those that are and those that are not synonymous? What empirical work does it do? Quine had argued 20 years earlier (Quine 1951) that the intuitive notion of synonymy had no clear empirical content, though one might of course devise artificial notions for this or that scientific purpose. Quine himself did just that with his 'stimulus synonymy' (Quine 1960: 31–5): on this admittedly minimal but empirically tractable conception (l) and (m) do have the same meaning (at any rate for all that the modal argument says).

So what notion of synonymy might support (13)? What empirical work does it do? How does it relate to the 'synonymy' that Frege or Russell *affirmed* between names and definite descriptions? Without answers to these questions it isn't just the soundness of Kripke's modal argument that is in jeopardy. The content of his conclusion, its bearing on his target and indeed its scientific interest must all remain open. Unfortunately Kripke says little to address these issues. To judge by his attitude towards philosophical 'intuitions' (NN:265–6/NN2:42) I suppose he means to rely on an 'intuitive' notion of meaning. But intuition does nothing to guide our judgement of the critical and questionable premise (13); 'intuitions' about meaning, on which *Naming and Necessity* frequently and heavily relies, let one down at this crucial point.

In conclusion: we saw two arguments for premise (1). The first argument can be defeated by scope considerations. The second, which was probably Kripke's, is unconvincing. Without a clearer specification of the content of 'meaning the same', its crucial premise remains open to doubt: so too, therefore, does (1) itself.

2.2.5 Its Second Premise

The second premise says that it isn't necessary that Aristotle was the teacher of Alexander. So stated, the premise appears to contain an ambiguity of scope: it might mean either of:

(n)   It is not necessary that: Aristotle was the teacher of Alexander
(o)   Aristotle is such that: it is not necessary that *he* was the teacher of Alexander

However, it is clear that while Kripke does indeed endorse (o) it is (n) that he has in mind:

> Not only is it true *of* the man Aristotle that he might not have gone into pedagogy; it is also true that we use the term 'Aristotle' in such a way that, in thinking of a counterfactual situation in which Aristotle didn't go into any of the fields and do any of the achievements we commonly attribute to him, still we should say that was a situation in which *Aristotle* did not do these things. (NN:279/NN2:62–3)

What grounds are there for this?

Kripke isn't entirely explicit; and it may be that our intuition that Aristotle might not have taught Alexander is better supported than any premises from which we can derive it. On the other hand, Kripke's modal argument is often represented as intimately involving *rigidity*: what stops a name from abbreviating a definite description is that the former is, and the latter isn't, rigid (Fitch

2004:37–8; Soames 2002:22). Now it may be that this is the basis of premise (2). We may sketch the argument as follows:

(16) 'Aristotle' designates rigidly (Premise)
(17) 'The teacher of Alexander' does not designate rigidly (Premise)
(18) 'Aristotle' refers to something and 'The teacher of Alexander' refers to nothing or something else at some possible world (from 16, 17)
(19) At some possible world Aristotle both existed and was not the teacher of Alexander (from 18)
(2) It is not necessary that: Aristotle (provided he existed) was the teacher of Alexander (from 19)

The question is: is there a sense of 'rigid' on which premises (16) and (17) are both true and strong enough to entail (18)?

Well, if 'rigid' means *persistently* rigid then it isn't clear that (16) and (17) do entail (18). It might be that (16) and (17) are both true and yet: at any possible world where Aristotle *exists*, 'The teacher of Alexander' denotes *him*; it is just that 'The teacher of Alexander' denotes somebody else at some possible world where Aristotle does *not* exist. But if 'rigid' means *mildly* rigid then (16) and (17) do entail (18). (16) entails that at every possible world where Aristotle exists, 'Aristotle' denotes him; (17) entails that at some possible world where Aristotle exists, 'The teacher of Alexander' does *not* denote him. Hence that world makes (18) true.

Now can we show that if 'rigidity' is understood as mild rigidity then premises (16) and (17) are *true*? A remark of Kripke's suggests the following intuitive test for rigidity (NN:346n25/NN2:62n25):

(p) A term t is rigid iff 'The thing that is in fact t might have both existed and failed to be t' is intuitively false

Note first that this tests for mild rigidity, not persistent rigidity.[6] But note also that 'Aristotle' passes this test and 'The teacher of Alexander' fails it. The thing that is in fact Aristotle could not have existed without being Aristotle; the thing that is in fact the teacher of Alexander (Aristotle) *could* have both existed and failed to be the teacher of Alexander. Hence premises (16) and (17) are both true and the argument for (2) is sound.

But note finally that if this is the basis on which we establish the rigidity of 'Aristotle' and the non-rigidity of 'The teacher of Alexander' then we can establish premise (2) without mentioning rigidity at all. We can instead proceed directly from the intuitions on which (16) and (17) were based:

(20) The thing that is in fact Aristotle could not have both existed and failed to be Aristotle (Premise)
(21) The thing that is in fact the teacher of Alexander could have both existed and failed to be the teacher of Alexander (Premise)
(22) Aristotle could have both existed and failed to be the teacher of Alexander (from 21[7])
(2) It is not necessary that: Aristotle (provided he existed) was the teacher of Alexander (from 20, 22)

The argument doesn't mention the rigidity of 'Aristotle' at all but proceeds directly from the intuitions that supported it. The fact, if it is one, that 'Aristotle' is rigid is therefore something of a red herring in the context of the modal argument. We do not at all need to have some notion of rigidity in mind in order to establish premise (2). All we need is the intuition that (20) and (21) are true. If 'rigidity' means *mild* rigidity then premises (16) and (17) are so to speak side-effects of that intuition.

There are two points to take from this. The first is that we saw an argument for the thesis that proper names are at least mildly rigid. The second is that even without this claim we can see that premise (2) is true.

2.2.6 Its Third Premise
The third premise says that if FRT is true then 'Aristotle' means the same as 'The teacher of Alexander'. You might deny this on the simple grounds that Kripke has chosen the wrong description: it may be that for most of us 'Aristotle' means instead something like 'The person who wrote *Nicomachean Ethics*' or perhaps 'The person generally *called* "Aristotle" '. That objection would be trifling. The validity of the modal argument and the truth of its other premises would be unaffected if we replaced any occurrence of 'The teacher of Alexander' with the preferred description.

What is not trifling is the suggestion that 'Aristotle' means the same as 'The *actual* teacher of Alexander'. As indicated at 2.2.1 the term 'the actual F' is used to specify whatever in *this* world satisfies the condition F. But if according to FRT 'Aristotle' means 'The *actual* teacher of Alexander' then premise (1) when suitably amended will be false: it isn't true that if 'Aristotle' means 'The actual teacher of Alexander' then 'Aristotle was the teacher of Alexander' is a necessary truth. For it isn't necessary that the actual teacher of Alexander (even provided that he existed) was the teacher of Alexander. On the contrary, if premise (2) is true then it might have been the case that the actual teacher of Alexander (i.e. Aristotle) never went into pedagogy at all.

Now it might be argued this defence isn't available to the *pure* version of FRT: that is, the thesis that names are synonymous with definite descriptions that do not themselves contain names, demonstratives or indexicals. One might argue that 'actually' is an indexical on the grounds that its reference, like that of the temporal qualifier 'present', depends on the location of the speaker: in particular, what possible world he is in when he says it. But this is hardly obvious. Unless you think that there really are concrete physical possible worlds somewhere in the universe corresponding to each possibility, it is simply not the case that any two speakers, however their situations might vary, ever use 'actual' to refer to different worlds. Even granting that 'actual' *is* indexical will raise no problems for the defender of IV/IVC, the *impure* version of FRT/ FRTC. And we saw that IV, not PV, is what the reasons for believing FRT motivated all along: see the arguments at 2.1.3 (i)–(v). Nothing in *those* arguments rules out that 'Aristotle' means the same as 'The *actual* such-and-such'. For example, consider the sceptical argument (v). The key point of (v) was that the meaning of an expression must be expressible in terms whose own meaningfulness is beyond doubt. The meaningfulness of 'actual' is as indubitable as those of 'here' and 'now' and at least as indubitable as that of 'I'.

So it appears that premise (3) is false.[8]

2.2.7 Conclusion

The modal argument against FRT is valid but not sound. Its second premise is intuitively plausible. But its first premise is questionable and its third premise is false. However, Kripke does have two other arguments against FRT and so we now turn to these.

2.3 THE SEMANTIC ARGUMENT

The semantic argument appears at NN:294–5/NN2:83–5. It says that if FRTC is true then whether or not a proper name refers to a thing depends on whether or not the thing satisfies the associated definite description. But in fact the reference of name to thing does *not* exhibit this pattern of dependence.

2.3.1 *What It Is*

In more detail the argument goes like this. Even if FRTC is true, and in general the meaning that one attaches to a name is given by a cluster of descriptions rather than just one, still there will be cases where one only knows *one* description that is uniquely satisfied by the bearer of the name.[9] Such is the case for many people with regard to the proper name 'Gödel'. Many of those who have heard of Gödel at all know just one thing about him – that he discovered the incompleteness of arithmetic. So even if FRTC is true in general it implies in this case – and clearly in many others too – that the name is associated with a *single* description that shares its meaning.

But then:

> Suppose that Gödel was not in fact the author of this theorem. A man named 'Schmidt', whose body was discovered in mysterious circumstances many years ago, actually did the work in question. His friend Gödel somehow got hold of the manuscript and it was thereafter attributed to Gödel. On the view in question [i.e. FRTC] ... when our ordinary man uses the name 'Gödel', he really means to refer to Schmidt. (NN:294/NN2:83–4)

But this consequence of FRTC is implausible.

Here the example is imaginary: it is possible that a speaker should associate a certain description with 'Gödel' and yet not be referring to whoever satisfies that description. There are actual examples too:

> Columbus was the first man to realize that the Earth was round. He was also the first European to land in the western hemisphere. Probably none of these things are true, and therefore, when people use the term 'Columbus' they really refer to some Greek if they use the roundness of the earth, or to some Norseman, perhaps, if they use the 'discovery of America'. But they

don't. So it does not seem that if most of the [associated descriptions] are satisfied by a unique object y, then y is the referent of that name. This seems simply to be false. (NN:295/NN2:85)

Using the example of 'Columbus', we may present the argument as follows:

(1) If FRT (or FRTC) is true then 'Columbus' means 'The first man to realize that the Earth was round' (Premise)
(2) If FRT (or FRTC) is true then 'Columbus' refers to whoever first realized that the Earth was round (from 1)
(3) If FRT (or FRTC) is true then 'Columbus' does not refer to Columbus (from 2)
(4) 'Columbus' refers to Columbus (Premise)
(5) FRT (and FRTC) is false (1, 5)

The argument is plainly valid given the additional premise that Columbus was *not* the first man to realize that the Earth was round. Are its premises true? I consider them together. The trouble with the argument isn't that one of them is obviously false but that they are in conflict.

2.3.2 Conflict between Its Premises

Recall first that we are concerned with a reading of FRTC on which what a *speaker* means by a name is given by descriptions that *he* associates with it (as discussed at 2.1.3(ii)). So premises (1) and (4) must be respectively that if FRTC is true then a *speaker's* term 'Columbus' means for him *Whoever first realized that the Earth was round* and that the speaker's term 'Columbus' refers to 'Columbus'. I argue (i) that for names – such as 'Columbus' – that meet a certain condition premise (1) is false. Then I argue (ii) that for names that do *not* meet the condition premise (4) is false.

(i) According to FRTC the meaning of a name is given by a set of associated descriptions that are accorded various weights (2.1.4). If premise (1) is true then we have a situation where 'The man who first realized that the Earth was round' has *maximal* weight. What does this mean? At 2.1.4 I characterized weight as follows: D1 carries greater weight than D2 does for a name N if 'D1 was F' is better grounds for asserting 'N was F' than 'D2 was not F' is for denying it. So to say that 'The first man to realize that the Earth was round' carries maximal weight is to say the following: for any *other* description D2 and for any predicate F, 'The first man to realize that the Earth was round was F' is better grounds for asserting 'Columbus was F' than is 'D2 was not F' for denying it.

But if this is what is meant by saying that 'Columbus' means *just* 'The first person to realize that the Earth was round' then that is *not* what 'Columbus' means for *anybody*. Let 'F' be the predicate 'Greek'; let D1 be the description 'The first man to realize that the Earth was round'; let D2 be the description 'The person that historians call "Columbus"' (assuming that Columbus in fact satisfies this description). The claim (a) 'D1 was F' is true, as is the claim (b) 'D2 was not F'; but *nobody* treats the truth of (a) as better grounds for asserting (c) 'Columbus was F' than is the truth of (b) for denying it. It is therefore plain that according to FRTC even ignorant speakers *do not* mean by 'Columbus' *just* what they mean by 'The first man to realize that the Earth was round'.

So what more do they mean by it? Well, they also believe that he is the person that *experts* call 'Columbus'.[10] And the facts just described show that the description 'The person whom historians call "Columbus"' carries some weight with respect to the name 'Columbus'. You would be prepared to revise your assent to 'Columbus was such-and-such' upon learning that the person historians call 'Columbus' was *not* such-and-such, notwithstanding your continued belief that the first person to realize the Earth was round *was* such-and-such. Hence there are at least *two* semantically active descriptions associated with 'Columbus': D1 and D2. The same point applies to Kripke's 'Gödel' example: the analogue of premise (1) is false here too. The reason is this. We all speak a common language and we are all aware that we do (how could we not be, given that we learn it from our fellow speakers?). It is because of this that linguistic use often requires *deference* to others. And this in turn motivates the thought that part (though only part) of the sense that we attach to a name is that of a description involving *other* speakers' (particularly experts') use of the name. That is ultimately why premise (1) and its analogues are false when applied to names known by their users to belong to a common language, e.g. 'Gödel' or 'Columbus'.

Now it might be objected that this appeal to descriptions

involving other speakers' use of the name is somehow unacceptable. Kripke in fact makes this objection and I consider it in the next section.

(ii) It might also be objected that even if 'Columbus' does not according to FRTC have as its whole meaning the definite description proposed by premise (1) we can still *imagine* names for which FRTC *does* have this consequence. Suppose e.g. that by 'James Watt' a speaker S means *only* what is meant by 'The inventor of the steam engine'. Suppose that S has no other beliefs about the referent of 'James Watt', or if he does they have no weight for him with respect to that name. In particular suppose that S either doesn't believe that the term has a common use; or he doesn't allow any facts about others' use of 'James Watt' to infringe upon his willingness to infer 'James Watt was F' from 'The inventor of the steam engine was F'. You and I know that (as *we* should say) James Watt was *not* the inventor of the steam engine – that was Hero of Alexandria.

Now if the facts about S are as described then it will be true to say that according to FRTC *his* expression 'James Watt' just means 'The inventor of the steam engine'. So in this case the relevant analogue of premise (1) is true. In light of these facts it is clear that S will be prepared in the light of historical discoveries to *reject* the sentence 'James Watt lived in the eighteenth century' and to *accept* the sentence 'James Watt lived in antique Alexandria'. But then shouldn't *we* say that *his* expression 'James Watt' refers *not* to James Watt but to Hero? What better evidence could there be for saying that an expression of an idiolect refers to Hero? But then the analogue of premise (4) is false. Somebody who uses 'James Watt' to mean *just* what is meant by 'The inventor of the steam engine' does *not* refer to James Watt but to somebody else.

In short there are two possibilities. Either 'Columbus' is knowingly used as part of a common language or (like 'James Watt') it isn't. In the first case the use of the term involves deference to expert usage. And this pattern of use makes it plausible that the meaning of the term involves more than just that of the single description 'The man who first realized that the Earth was round'. And so in the first case premise (1) is false, even for ignorant speakers. In the second case premise (1) may be true. But as we have just seen from the 'James Watt' example, the application of premise (1) implies a pattern of use that makes it implausible that 'Columbus' so used refers to Columbus rather than to some Greek philosopher. And then premise (4) is false.

It remains to address the unfinished business at the end of part (i) of this argument. I said that the description 'The person called "Columbus"' is something that a speaker might associate with 'Columbus'. It remains to be seen whether this view faces further objections.

2.3.3 Circularity and Passing the Buck

It is important to be clear that Kripke's objection to the proposal that *some* of us associate with 'Columbus' the description 'The man called "Columbus"' is *not* that it is circular. That impression can easily arise from the following passage:

> Someone uses the name 'Socrates'. How are we supposed to know to whom he refers? By using the description which gives the sense of it. According to Kneale, the description is 'the man called "Socrates"'. And here ... it tells us nothing at all. Taking it in this way seems to be no theory of reference at all. We ask 'To whom does he refer by "Socrates"?' And then the answer is given 'Well, he refers to the man to whom he refers.' If this were all there was to the meaning of a proper name then no reference would get off the ground at all. (NN:284/NN2:70)

The following theories might face this objection: (a) The theory that by 'Socrates' each of us means 'The person whom *I* call "Socrates"'; (b) The theory that by 'Socrates' each of us means 'The person whom everyone *else* calls "Socrates"'; (c) The theory that by 'Socrates' A means 'The person that B calls "Socrates"' and B means 'The person that C calls "Socrates"' and ... and Z means 'The person that A calls "Socrates"'. In each of these cases the reference of 'Socrates' isn't fixed. Such a situation as (c) *could* arise if we were unlucky enough (through misunderstandings, Chinese whispers etc. – for an example see Kroon 1989: 376) but it doesn't arise for most proper names.

But the proposal at 2.3.2(i) doesn't face this objection. The proposal is that most of us (non-experts) associate with 'Columbus' the description 'The man called "Columbus" by historians'. It is *not* that the experts themselves mean by 'Columbus' either 'The person that non-experts call "Columbus"' or 'The person that experts call

"Columbus" '. In that case the account would again be circular. The proposal is rather that at one end of the 'reference-borrowing' chain there are people who associate with 'Columbus' a description that does *not* appeal to any facts about what other speakers refer to.[11]

Kripke's objection is stated most clearly in an addendum to the second edition of *Naming and Necessity*. There he writes:

> The objection to such non-circular determinations of reference as 'Let "Glumph" be the man Jones calls "Glumph" ' and, 'Let Gödel be the man to whom the experts attribute the incompleteness theorem' (said by a layman) is otherwise: In general, a speaker cannot be sure from whom he picked up his reference; and as far as he knows 'the experts' may well realize that Schmidt, not Gödel, proved the incompleteness theorem even though the inexpert speaker still attributes it to Gödel. Thus such determinations of the referent may well give the wrong result, and the speaker surely cannot be said to know *a priori* ... that they do not. (NN2:161)

The proposal at 2.3.2(i) was that by 'Columbus' we laymen mean (in part) what is meant by 'The man the experts call "Columbus" '. As is clear from this passage, Kripke's objection is that we laymen cannot be sure 'from whom we picked up our reference'.

It isn't clear that the objection succeeds. Even if I have forgotten everything about the person from whom I first *got* the name 'Columbus' it still doesn't follow that I cannot *now* mean by it something like 'The person whom the experts call "Columbus" '. What I *now* mean by the name is exhibited in the way I go about assessing sentences involving 'Columbus': this will include appeals to expert authorities but it won't include any attempt to recollect how I learnt the name. The fact that I cannot remember who I learnt it from (as I actually have) is therefore irrelevant to the meaning that I now associate with that name.[12]

On the other hand the objection was perhaps never intended to apply to the proposal at 2.3.2(i). We can see this if we grasp a distinction that has hitherto been irrelevant. Kripke distinguishes the theory that the *meaning* of a name is that of a definite description from the theory that the description *fixes the reference* of the name (NN:258–60/NN2:31–4). The latter does *not* say that the name is synonymous with the description. It only says that we use the description to specify the thing that the name in fact refers to. Thus if somebody asks me what 'John Smith' refers to I might point to someone and say 'The man over there'. Here, 'The man over there' fixes the referent of 'John Smith' but doesn't give its meaning: you might come to grasp the meaning of the name and yet forget how it had been introduced to you. Let us call these two theories the *synonymy theory* and the *reference-fixing theory* respectively. FRTC is a version of the former.

Kripke thinks that it is a distinctive consequence of the synonymy theory that the referent of a name necessarily has the properties attributed to it by the associated definite description (NN:276–7/NN2:57–8). The modal argument is of course an argument against that consequence of the theory. Since Kripke regards the modal argument as having disposed of the synonymy theory, only the reference-fixing theory remains. But Kripke also thinks that the reference-fixing theory is false (NN:277/NN2:59). And the objection in the passage just quoted is an objection to *that* theory. At any rate it makes more sense in that light. The passage *does* raise a legitimate point against a reference-fixing theory: if I cannot recall whom I got the reference of the name from then I cannot use 'The person called "Columbus" by such-and-such' as a device for *specifying* what 'Columbus' in fact refers to.

If the synonymy theory (i.e. FRTC) had indeed been finished off by the modal objection then this would be a legitimate objection to the remaining theory that the reference of a name is fixed by, though its meaning isn't given by, a definite description. But the synonymy theory has not been finished off by the modal argument. Against the version of *that* theory that makes 'The man called "Columbus" by experts' part of the meaning I attach to 'Columbus', Kripke's present objection is not (and perhaps was not intended to be) effective.

2.3.4 Conclusion

The semantic argument is not sound. If a name is knowingly used as part of a common language its premise (1) is false: it is part of the meaning of a name that it refers to what experts use it to refer to. If the name is not so used premise (4) is false: in an idiolect whose speaker means by 'Columbus' *just* 'The first man to realize that the Earth was round' the name 'Columbus' does *not* refer to Columbus.

2.4 THE EPISTEMOLOGICAL ARGUMENT

The epistemological argument against FRTC is stated very briefly at NN:296/NN2:87. It is obviously different from the modal argument and subtly different from the semantic one. Partly the confusion might arise from the fact that Kripke uses the 'Gödel' example for both. The distinction is as follows. The semantic argument says that it *need* not be the case that the referent of a name satisfies the associated descriptions. The epistemological argument says that even if it *is* the case we do not know it *a priori*, contrary to FRTC.

2.4.1 What It Is

The argument runs as follows. If FRTC is true then one ought to know *a priori* that Gödel (if he existed) satisfied at least some of the descriptions associated with 'Gödel': it could not turn out that this is in fact false. But we do not know this *a priori*: it isn't ruled out that experience should lead us to deny it. What was presented in the semantic argument as a blatant fantasy (that Gödel did not discover the incompleteness theorem) is hardly false *a priori*. We cannot rule out future evidence that shows it to have been Schmidt.

We can write the argument as follows:

(1) It is not known *a priori* that Gödel (if he existed) discovered the incompleteness theorem (Premise)
(2) If FRTC is true then it *is* known *a priori* that Gödel (if he existed) discovered the incompleteness theorem (Premise)
(3) FRTC is false (from 1, 2)

As presented, the argument is valid. As with the semantic argument, I shall examine its premises not severally but together. The premises are in conflict: the grounds for believing the first premise are grounds for rejecting the second.

2.4.2 Conflict Between Its Premises

Start by focusing on premise (1). The grounds for believing this are grounds for thinking that it might turn out, contrary to what we all thought, that Gödel did not in fact discover the incompleteness theorem.

How could this happen? Well, we could imagine evidence appearing for the scenario described at 2.3.1. Reports are unearthed of Schmidt's body having been found in Vienna; in one of his pockets was a manuscript, in his own handwriting, of what we thought was Gödel's proof of the incompleteness theorem. The manuscript predates Gödel's publication of the theorem, it is known that Schmidt and Gödel were good friends, etc.

But why are we prepared to regard this as evidence that *Gödel* did not prove the incompleteness of arithmetic rather than evidence that Gödel was in fact Schmidt? Well, one reason might be that we associate with the name 'Gödel' descriptions other than just 'the discoverer of the incompleteness theorem'. We also associate with that name such descriptions as 'The person known as "Gödel" by his friends' and 'The discoverer of the completeness of first-order logic', etc. But if that is the explanation then premise (2) is false: the proponent of FRTC can say that these other descriptions carry some weight with respect to 'Gödel': so even on his view it is hardly *a priori* that Gödel discovered the incompleteness of arithmetic.

Suppose then that nobody knows *anything* to specify Gödel other than that he discovered the incompleteness of arithmetic. So there are no other descriptions that we can attach to the name 'Gödel'. Is it still possible that we should find evidence that Gödel both existed and wasn't the discoverer of the incompleteness theorem?

According to Kripke the answer is yes. In defence of this he gives another example, that of the character Jonah. We know nothing about Jonah other than what is related of him in the Bible:

> [W]hile biblical scholars generally hold that Jonah did exist, the account not only of his being swallowed by a big fish but even going to Nineveh to preach or anything else that is said in the biblical story is substantially false. But nevertheless there are reasons for thinking this was about a real prophet ... there are independent reasons for thinking that this was not a pure legend about an imaginary character but one about a real character. (NN:282/NN2:67)

So: here we have a case where *everything* we thought we knew about Jonah is false: but these are still regarded as fictions about a real person rather than fictions about an imaginary person. And what holds for Jonah holds for Gödel: it isn't *a priori* that he did *any* of the things that have been said of him, and hence not *a priori*, contrary to FRTC, that he satisfied *any* of the descriptions associated with his name.

But what reason could there be for saying that the story is a fiction about a real person rather than a fiction about an imaginary person? If *nobody* did *any* of those things then what reason is there for saying that these are fictions about the doings of *this* bearded 'prophet' rather than *that* one? And if there are none, why are they about *any* real person?

The only reason I can see for describing the fiction as being *about* some real person is this: that there was some one real person whose doings were in some way the *causal source* of the fiction or at any rate of most of it. Were that not the case – i.e. if *many* people's doings were variously sources of the legend or if *nobody's* doings were – then the legend would not be about *anyone*.

But if that is the reason for calling the legend a fiction about a real person then these grounds for premise (1) may tell against premise (2). If the legend doesn't have a single causal source then it cannot be said to be about anyone and therefore cannot be cited in support of premise (1). But if it *does* have such a source we may conjecture that there is another description that the supporter of FRTC can incorporate into the meaning of 'Jonah': namely, *the causal source of the legend.* But then it seems that premise (2) is false: it is not for FRTC *a priori* that Jonah (or Gödel) did any of the things related of him because it isn't *a priori* that the causal source of those stories did any of the things that they relate of him.[13]

But *do* speakers associate the description 'The causal source of our information involving N' with the name N? How are we to settle this question? One source of evidence might be facts about the way speakers revise what they say in the face of new information. And here the very evidence that supported premise (1) seems also to support this conjecture. Consider again the case of Jonah. The evidence seems to be that *nobody* was swallowed by a whale or did any of the other things that the Bible relates of Jonah; but there *was* a single man whose doings were responsible for these legends. This is why scholars will say: 'Jonah existed but did none of the things related of him'. Now isn't the fact *that* scholars describe the situation in this way evidence that their use of 'Jonah' is being *guided* by the description 'the source of these legends'? And isn't that evidence – what better evidence is wanted? – that that description is part of the cluster they *associate* with 'Jonah'? And the same may be said about 'Gödel': if premise (1) is true then that can only be because we have some other way of picking out Gödel than as the discoverer of the incompleteness of arithmetic. But if we do have some other way of doing so then it is open to the defender of FRTC to incorporate this into the description associated with 'Gödel'. And this in turn means that premise (2) is false. If this is the position then it looks as though the grounds for the first premise of the epistemological argument do after all undermine the second.

2.4.3 Conclusion

The epistemological argument is valid but not sound. The same is true of it as was true of the semantic argument: our reasons for believing the first premise are reasons for doubting the second. It is hardly surprising that a defender of FRTC should find the same problem with both arguments. In both cases one premise sought to show that some set of descriptions D associated with the name 'Gödel' may in some circumstances be dissociated from its referent. But if it is intuitive that there *are* such circumstances then it is plausible that our intuitions are in those circumstances guided by some *further* beliefs that we have about 'Gödel'. But FRTC can then incorporate those further beliefs into the descriptions associated with 'Gödel': what is it other than the *meaning* of a name that guides your *use* of that name in given circumstances? This falsifies the other premise of both arguments that the set D by itself exhausts the descriptions that for FRTC determine the meaning of 'Gödel'.

2.5 SUMMARY

FRT as originally introduced is plainly false for the reasons stated at 2.1.4. Its successor FRTC does however have a chance of being true. We considered three Kripkean arguments against it: the modal argument, the semantic argument and the epistemological argument. The modal argument may force us to drop the *pure* version PVC of FRTC for the reasons stated at 2.2.6. But IVC remains faithful to the motivation stated at 2.1.3, to which moreover none of the other arguments generate any further resistance.

3

NECESSITY

The material from NN:302/NN2:97 to the end of the third lecture of *Naming and Necessity* covers four important topics: (i) essential properties of individuals; (ii) essential and *a priori* properties of natural kinds; (iii) modal illusion; (iv) materialism in the philosophy of mind. The issues are related. For example many of the arguments that fall under (ii) correspond to arguments under (i). And the anti-materialistic arguments that fall under (iv) draw on considerations drawn from each of (i)–(iii).

3.1 ESSENTIAL PROPERTIES OF INDIVIDUALS

Kripke makes the following claims concerning essential properties: that his ancestry is essential to a person; that its material origin is essential to an artefact; and that its material constitution is essential to a physical object. Before we describe and assess his arguments we must consider more closely what sense there is in the distinction between essential and accidental properties.

3.1.1 Does the Distinction Make Sense?

It is possible to distinguish *essential* and *accidental* properties of an object. An *essential* property of a is one that a could not have lacked if it existed at all. (It isn't metaphysically possible that a both existed and lacked that property.) An accidental property is one that a might have lacked while still existing. It may e.g. be said that Richard Nixon essentially has the property of being human: *he* could not have existed without being human. But it is an accidental property of Nixon that he was President in 1970: there is some possible world where Nixon both exists and isn't then President.

It has been objected that the distinction between essential and accidental properties is not one between properties of an individual but only between properties of an individual *relative to a certain description or background grouping*. Thus Quine:

> Mathematicians may conceivably be said to be necessarily rational and not necessarily two-legged; and cyclists necessarily two-legged and not necessarily rational. But what of an individual who counts among his eccentricities both mathematics and cycling? Is this concrete individual necessarily rational and not necessarily two-legged or vice versa? Just in so far as we are talking referentially of the object, with no special bias towards a background grouping of mathematicians as against cyclists, or vice versa, there is no semblance of sense in rating some of his attributes [i.e. properties] as necessary and others as contingent. (Quine 1960: 199)

Relative to the background grouping of mathematicians it both makes sense and is true to say that this individual is necessarily rational. He could not have belonged to the group if he had not been rational. And relative to the background grouping of cyclists it both makes sense and is true to say that this individual is accidentally rational: he could have been an irrational cyclist. But it makes no sense to say that this individual considered just as such is e.g. necessarily rational or accidentally bipedal. Therefore we cannot say *sans phrase* that a *thing* has accidental or essential properties but only it has them relative to a certain description.

Kripke's reply is that it makes *intuitive* sense to say that a thing has such properties:

> Suppose that someone said, pointing to Nixon, 'That's the guy who might have lost'. Someone else says 'Oh no, if you describe him as "Nixon", then he might have lost; but, of course, describing him as the winner, then it is not true that he might have lost'. Now which one is being the philosopher, here, the unintuitive man? It seems to me obviously to be the second. The second man has a philosophical theory. The first man would say, and with great conviction, 'Well, of course, the winner of the election *might have been someone else* ... On the other hand the term "Nixon" is just a *name* of *this man*'. When you ask whether

it is necessary or contingent that *Nixon* won the election, you are asking the intuitive question whether in some counterfactual situation, *this man* would in fact have lost the election. If someone thinks that the notion of a necessary ... property ... is a philosopher's notion with no intuitive content, he is wrong. (NN:265/NN2:41–2).

The point is essential to Kripke's case for saying that proper names are rigid and also in arguing for the second premise of the modal argument against FRT.[1] So it is important to him that things can intuitively be said to have accidental or necessary properties.

There are three points to make about this important passage.

(i) It may indeed be intuitively acceptable to point to someone and say '*He*'s the man who might have lost'. But it doesn't follow that when we are saying this we are ascribing an accidental property to that person regardless of any background grouping that might have been presupposed. Such a grouping might indeed form a background assumption whenever we speak about what might have happened to a man. Suppose I said to Kripke's naïve subject: 'When you say "*He* might have lost" do you mean (a) that possibly someone with Nixon's name, career, origins, appearance and political views loses? Or do you mean (b) that possibly *he himself* loses?' It is easy to imagine the reply that *either* formulation captures the content (or at any rate the point) of what he was getting at. It is also possible to imagine him shrugging his shoulders and saying '*You're* the philosopher. *You* tell *me*.'

No doubt *some* philosophically apathetic or ignorant subjects would insist that it was (b) they were getting at. But we might suspect that even what *they* mean (if anything) is compatible with (a). It is intuitively natural to say 'I might have been Napoleon', because you can imagine e.g. what you would have done if you had *been* Napoleon. And it is natural to insist that what one imagines is that oneself – *this very person* – is Napoleon. But a little reflection will show that they are not so much imagining a situation where someone actually distinct from Napoleon is identical to him (which Kripke himself regards as impossible – see NN:350–1n56/NN2:114n56; see also Williams 1966) but rather one where Napoleon has the imaginer's character traits and perhaps beliefs. But if we are entitled to reconstrue the intuition expressed by 'I myself – *this very person* – might have been Napoleon' as making tacit appeal to certain descriptions of myself (my personality etc.) then why are we prohibited from reconstruing the intuition expressed by 'Nixon himself – *this very person* – might have lost' in the same way?

(ii) The contrary appearance may arise from ambiguity in the use of italics or emphasis. Emphasis may be used not to alter the content of what is said but only to draw your attention to some part of it ('I said turn *left*'). At other times emphasis affects what is meant ('Will you be alive in 20 years' time?' sounds like a question about your health; 'Will *you* be alive in 20 years' time?' sounds like one about personal identity). The appearance that the essential/accidental distinction is meaningful may arise from a confusion of these.

Consider the following three sentences:

(a)   When I say 'Nixon might have lost' I am saying that this man might have lost
(b)   When I say 'Nixon might have lost' I am saying that *this man* might have lost
(c)   When I say 'Nixon might have lost' I am saying that winning is an accidental property of Nixon himself, regardless of how you describe him

Now in everyday contexts the emphasis in (b) will be understood not as changing the content of (a) but merely as directing your attention to a part of it, e.g. if you took me to be pointing at someone else. But in philosophical contexts we use it to say something different from (a): we use it to say something that implies (c). And it doesn't follow that (c) inherits any intuitive plausibility from (a). All we can say is this. If the italicization is being used as an attention-director then (b) means the same as (a); both are intuitively plausible but neither implies (c). If the italicization is being used as a content-specifier then (c) follows from (b). But then (b) is neither intuitively plausible nor a consequence of (a). It is only when we confuse these two interpretations of the italics that (c) appears to follow from the intuitive (a): in fact it doesn't.

(iii) In any case, even if Kripke is correct that the accidental/essential distinction *does* make intuitive sense, why should we respect the intuition? That it makes sense to a non-philosopher who hasn't thought about it is no grounds for dismissing the contrary view of a philosopher who *has* thought about it. Kripke's own view

(NN:265–6/NN2:42) is that in this area intuitions are the most conclusive evidence that you can get. There are other philosophers who have accorded special authority to intuitions – I suppose Aristotle is the outstanding example. But what distinguishes Aristotle is the fact that he *based* this attitude towards intuitions on a background theory: his (highly *un*intuitive!) philosophy of mind.[2] Kripke on the contrary appears to have no grounds at all for trusting intuition. It would be preferable to take Hume's attitude that while our intuitions are perhaps unavoidable outside of the study, this confers no philosophical authority upon them.

To summarize: Quine cast doubt on whether it makes sense to speak of accidental or essential properties of an individual *sans phrase*. Kripke replied that it makes intuitive sense. But this is doubtful. And even if it *does* seem to intuition that it makes sense, why should we respect this? Be that as it may, I will follow Kripke and most other philosophers in assuming that it *does* make sense to call a property essential or accidental. Let us now consider Kripke's views as to which ones can *truly* be called essential.

3.1.2 Essentiality of Human Ancestry
Kripke thinks that a person could not have had parents other than his actual ones. He denies e.g. that Queen Elizabeth II could have been born of Mr and Mrs Harry Truman (rather than George VI and Elizabeth Bowes-Lyon).

What direct support Kripke gives for this claim appears in the following passage:

> [C]an we imagine a situation in which it would have happened that this very woman came out of Mr and Mrs Truman? They might have had a child resembling her in many properties. Perhaps in some possible world Mr and Mrs Truman even had a child who actually became the Queen of England and was even passed off as the child of other parents. This still would not be a situation in which *this very woman* whom we call 'Elizabeth II' was the child of Mr and Mrs Truman, or so it seems to me. It would be a situation in which there was some other woman who had many of the properties that are in fact true of Elizabeth ... How could a person originating from different parents, from a totally different sperm and egg, be *this very woman*? (NN:313–4/ NN2:112–3)

What is striking about this passage is that it is difficult to find an argument in it. Kripke simply *asserts* that any world where the Trumans have a daughter, who otherwise resembles the actual Elizabeth as much as you like, is still not a world where *Elizabeth* is the Trumans' daughter but one where somebody resembling her is. That is his intuition.

Should we trust this intuition? I think there are two reasons for *not* trusting it. Both are independent of the general suspicion of intuition recommended at 3.1.1(iii).

First: intuitions about what could or might have been the case are highly sensitive to the line of questioning that elicits them. If I ask (a) 'Would it have been *that very woman*, if the Trumans had had a daughter who resembled Elizabeth II in all other respects and who became Queen of England?' you would probably say no. But if I simply said without emphasis (b) 'Could Elizabeth II have had different parents?' you would probably say yes. The reason for the difference is plausibly that the emphasis in (a) functions as a means of introducing tighter criteria for what kind of thing can count as *the same woman* as Elizabeth II; being a co-operative conversational partner you acquiesce in this tightening and therefore answer no to (a) (for other instances of this phenomenon see Lewis 1979 esp. vol. 1: 246–7). Now it might be argued that it is only *strict* identity across possible worlds that concerns Kripke, so he is right to go by our intuitive responses under the tightest criteria, i.e. those elicited by questions involving emphasis. But then here is another case where emphasis has a similar tightening effect: 'If you had been brought up in a different culture then would you *really* have been *the very same person*?' elicits the intuitive answer no. And yet Kripke would not say that I could not have been brought up in a different culture.

The second reason not to trust Kripke's intuition that one could not have had different parents is that intuitions to the contrary not only *exist* but also matter as much as modal intuitions ever do. Amongst the practical uses of modal judgement are the justification of regret and the allocation of blame. But someone who is thinking about what he regrets will find it the most natural thing in the world to say that he might have had different parents. The son of a peasant might regret not having been the son of the Duke of Westminster. One might say 'If I had been the son of the King I'd have had more opportunities in my life' (cf. Mellor 1977:310). One might indeed be motivated by this regret to act in a way that one otherwise would not have done – perhaps Danton was. Doesn't this entirely intuitive regret presuppose that one *might* have had different parents? It seems therefore that we have two clashing intuitions: the intuition that one might have had different parents and the Kripkean intuition that one could not. But this conflict isn't itself a reason to drop the first intuition. Even somebody who possessed both intuitions and became aware of the conflict between them would probably still be motivated by the first. Doesn't this show that we are more deeply committed to the first intuition than to the second?

Of course Kripke might reply that what Danton *really* meant by 'I might have had different parents' is only that his actual parents might have led more prosperous lives than they actually did, or that he might have been switched at birth, or something like that. But this isn't the face value of the intuition; and what are Kripke's grounds for not taking it at face value other than *another* intuition? But then the position is this: sometimes we have modal intuitions that one could *not* have had different parents; at other times we have practically potent intuitions to the contrary. Kripke's preference for reconstruing the intuition of contingency appears either unmotivated or based on a prior belief that in fact one's ancestry *is* essential: but the ground for this was supposed to be the very intuitions that the belief is now being invoked to defend! In the first case his position is arbitrary; in the second case his argument for it is circular.[3]

So if Kripke's argument for the essentiality of ancestry is meant to be intuitive then we ought not to accept it.

In a passage elided from the above quotation Kripke remarks that when considering alternative possibilities 'one is given ... a previous history of the world, and from that time it diverges considerably from the actual course'. And this suggests a second argument for the essentiality of ancestry:

> It may truly be said of President Nixon, for instance, that he might never have been a politician, because there was a time in his life at which it would have been true to say that he might never become a politician. It is in just this sense that we can say that St Anne might never have married ... But we cannot push back the moment in respect of which a property is to be

characterized as [something it might come not to possess] behind the point at which the object came into existence. (Dummett 1981a: 131; see also Mackie 1974)

In short: it can truly be said of N that he might not have had some property P that he actually has only if at some time in the past it was true that N might *in the future* fail to have P. But if N's parents were A and B then there *was* no time in the past when it would have been true to say that N might *in the future* fail to have A and B as parents: not after N was conceived, because then no possibility remains of changing his parentage; but not before either, because we cannot say truly of something that doesn't yet exist that it might fail to have A and B as parents.

I am not sure that Kripke had this argument in mind, for he expresses ambivalence about the principle behind it (NN:351n57(1)/ NN2:115n57(1)). But in any case it appears to prove too much. The supposed reason for saying that one's ancestry is essential to one's identity would seem also to show that the *location* as well as the time of one's conception is essential to it. But surely one's conception might have occurred in some place other than where it actually occurred. Suppose e.g. that you were conceived on an aeroplane; just prior to the moment of conception the pilot accidentally veered out of Russian and into Chinese airspace. Then you were conceived in China but might have been conceived in Russia. So there must be something wrong with this argument.

In conclusion: we saw two grounds for Kripke's claim that your ancestry is essential. The first was intuition: but the contrary intuition is equally strong and more practically potent. The second was the temporal argument just considered: but this ought not to be trusted because as well as the essentiality of ancestry its premises have other less palatable consequences.

3.1.3 Essentiality of Material Origin
Could this table have been made out of some block of wood entirely distinct from the one it was actually made from? More generally, if a material object had its actual origin in a certain piece of matter then could it have originated in some entirely distinct piece of matter? Kripke thinks not. In support of this he doesn't just offer intuition but also a definite argument. The argument is framed without loss of generality in terms of tables and pieces of wood:

Let 'B' be a name (rigid designator) of a table, let 'A' name the piece of wood from which it actually came. Let 'C' name another piece of wood. Then suppose B were made from A, as in the actual world, but also another table D were simultaneously made from C. (We assume there is no relation between A and C which makes the possibility of making a table from one dependent on the possibility of making a table from the other.) Now in this situation $B \neq D$; hence, even if D were made by itself and no table were made from A, D would not be B. (NN:350n56/ NN2:114n56)

Let us write this out in numbered steps:

(1) Table B is made from block A (Supposition)
(2) If it is possible to make one of tables B and D from blocks A and C respectively then it is possible to make both (Premise)
(3) At every possible world where D is made from C, $D \neq B$ (Premise)
(4) At some possible world w table B is made from block A and table D is made from some distinct block C (from 1, 2)
(5) At w, D and B are distinct (from 3, 4)
(6) At any possible world where B exists and D is made from C, D and B are distinct (from 5, necessity of distinctness)
(7) At any possible world where B exists and *anything* is made from C, it is distinct from B (from 6)
(8) At every possible world B is not made from C (from 7)
(9) If table B is made from block A then it cannot have been made from block C (from 8, discharging 1)

Since C was an arbitrary block of wood wholly distinct from A it follows that B could not have been made from *any* other block of wood (or other material) than A. Steps (7)–(9) are not made explicit but it is reasonable to expect that Kripke had something like them in mind. Certainly (9) is the intended conclusion; and if (6) is not thought to entail (7) then it is unclear how we are supposed to get from (6) to (9). The step from (5) to (6) relies on the (necessary) necessity of distinctness: if D and B are distinct at a possible world then they are not identical at *any* possible world (perhaps because at least one of them fails to exist). I consider that assumption at 3.1.6.

Even if we assume that the step from (5) to (6) is valid, the argument as a whole is still *in*valid. This will appear if we consider the following formally identical argument:

(10) Person B^* is married to person A^* (Supposition)
(11) If it is possible to marry one of persons B^* and D^* to persons A^* and C^* respectively then it is possible to marry both (Premise)
(12) At every possible world where D^* is married to C^*, $D^* \neq B^*$ (Premise)
(13) At some possible world w person B^* is married to person A^* and person D^* is married to some distinct person C^* (from 10, 11)
(14) At w, D^* and B^* are distinct (from 12, 13)
(15) At any possible world where B^* exists and D^* is married to C^*, D^* and B^* are distinct (from 14, necessity of distinctness)
(16) At any possible world where B^* exists and *anyone* is married to C^*, he is distinct from B^* (from 15)
(17) At every possible world B^* is not married to C^* (from 16)
(18) If B^* is married to A^* then he cannot have been married to C^* (from 17, discharging 10)

This argument is formally equivalent to the first and its premises are equally plausible. But its absurd conclusion is that nobody could have been married to anyone other than the person he is in fact married to. So there must be something wrong with the argument. But then there will be a corresponding fault in Kripke's argument.

It is easy to identify the difficulty: the step from (15) to (16). Even if it is true as (15) says that D^* cannot have been married to C^* and been the same person as B^*, it does *not* follow that B^* could not have been married to C^*. The corresponding step of Kripke's argument is that from (6) to (7): even though table D cannot have been made from block C and been the same table as B, it doesn't follow that table B could not have been made from block C. Why could there not be a possible world where table B is distinct from table D and yet for all that fashioned from block C?

The step from (6) to (7) can be made valid if we add this premise: at any possible world where a table is made from C that table is D, or in short:

(19) Only table D could have been made from block C

Clearly (7) follows from (6) *and* (19). For it follows from (19) that no table could have been both distinct from D and fashioned from C and hence by (6) that table B could not have been fashioned from C. Moreover no analogue of (19) applies to the argument concerning marriage: it isn't true that only person D^* could have been married to C^*. (19) is the converse of Kripke's intended conclusion (9); we may call it the thesis of the *sufficiency of material origin*.

The trouble is that (19) is at least as questionable as the conclusion of the argument. Why could I not make some *other* table than D from block C? If the person who made D (or somebody else) had fashioned a table of different height from D's actual height, in a different style and using different instruments, then why would it not have been a different table?

In conclusion Kripke's argument for the necessity of material origin is invalid. It can be made valid if we assume the *sufficiency* of material origin. But the sufficiency of material origin is at least as questionable as its necessity.[4]

3.1.4 Essentiality of Material Constitution

As well as the material from which an artefact originated, Kripke also thinks that the material out of which an object is *originally constituted* is essential to it (NN:350n57/NN2:114–5n57; NN:321–2/NN2:126–7).

This question of original constitution must be distinguished from two others. (i) It isn't the question of what constitution a thing must have in the *future* if it then exists. It may be that this wooden table could not survive as a table constituted of ice: were it to turn to ice it would cease to exist. But this isn't the same as saying that it must (at all times in its existence) have been *originally* constituted of wood rather than ice. (ii) It isn't the question just considered: the question of what object it must have been made *from*. Even if it is true that this table must have been made from that block of wood, it doesn't follow that the table must have been (or even is actually) *constituted* of wood at the moment when it first came into existence. (It might have been made by some lengthy process that as well as shaping the wood into a table turned it into coal.) The question is this: given that the table was in fact constituted of a certain material at the first moment of its existence, could it have been constituted of something else at that moment?

Kripke argues that the answer is no in two places. In the first place he appears to be arguing from the premise (discussed at 3.1.3) that the table could not have been made from raw materials different from its actual raw materials:

> Obviously this question is related to the necessity of the origin of the table from a given block of wood and whether that block, too, is essentially wood (even wood of a particular kind). Thus it is ordinarily impossible to imagine the table made from any substance other than the one of which it is actually made without going back through the entire history of the universe, a mind-boggling feat. (NN:351n57/NN2:114–15n57)

I understand this as follows. Any world where the table is originally constituted of e.g. stone must differ from actuality over what its raw materials were constituted of. But if *those* raw materials were constituted of something different from what they were actually constituted of then the materials from which *they* originated would have to have had a different original constitution from their actual constitution too. And so on back forever: assuming that there is a minimum length of time for each step of the process this implies that any such possible world would have to differ from @ throughout its history. We may write the argument like this:

(20) No object could have been made from any raw materials other than the ones that it was actually made from (Premise)

(21) If this wooden table had originally been constituted of something other than wood then its actual raw materials would have to have been constituted of something other than what *they* were actually constituted of (from 20)

(22) No raw materials could have been constituted of anything other than what they were actually constituted of unless the materials that *they* originated from were previously constituted of something other than what they were actually constituted of (from 20)

(23) If this wooden table had originally been constituted of something other than wood then the entire history of the universe would have been different (21, 22)

I said that Kripke doesn't give convincing grounds for the premise of this argument. But even if we grant that premise, the argument is still invalid: neither (21) nor (22) follows from (20). Imagine the following production process. A block B of metallic material M is turned into a wooden table T through being heated and shaped. If B is heated to a certain temperature K then its material M turns into wood; but if B is heated to some temperature *higher* than K then M turns into *stone*. (The example is fantastic if we consider these particular materials; but there are other materials for which it is not.) Now even if T could not have been made from any block other than B, it is *not* the case that if T had originally been constituted of stone then B wouldn't have had its actual constitution M. It could have been that T was originally made of stone because the *same* block B made from the *same* material M had been heated to a temperature higher than K. And so (21) doesn't follow from (20); for the same reason neither does (22).

In the second place Kripke gives intuitive motivations for the essentiality of constitution:

> The vicissitudes of *this thing* [a table] might have been very different from its actual history. It might have been transported to the Kremlin. It might have already been hewn into bits and no longer exist at the present time. Various things might have happened to it. But whatever we imagine counterfactually having happened to it other than what actually did, the one thing we cannot imagine happening to this thing is that *it*, given that it is composed of molecules, should still have existed and not have been composed of molecules. (NN:321–2/NN2:126–7)

This is simply an appeal to intuition. And it faces the difficulties raised at 3.1.1 against appeals to intuitions in general and those raised at 3.1.2 against the intuitive argument for the essentiality of ancestry: for example it is very easy to imagine saying 'If this thing had not been composed of molecules then it would not have behaved in such-and-such way'. I won't repeat those arguments here.

In conclusion, Kripke's two arguments for the essentiality of constitution are unconvincing. The first was that a possible world where an object has a different original constitution from its actual one will differ from @ throughout its history. The second was that the thesis was intuitively compelling. But the first argument was invalid. And the intuitions behind the second, even if they exist, are not compelling.

3.1.5 Necessity of Identity and Distinctness

If s and t are identical then could they have been distinct? If s and t are distinct then could they have been identical? Kripke thinks the answer to both questions is no. He *also* thinks that ordinary identity statements of English such as 'George Orwell = Eric Blair' have their truth-values necessarily.

Before considering his arguments for the first two claims we must distinguish three things that they each might mean. Let s and t be names or other referring expressions and consider the following three sentences:

(a) If $s = t$ then s and t are such that necessarily: if either exists then they are identical

(b) If $s = t$ then s is such that necessarily: if it exists then it is identical to t

(c) If $s = t$ then necessarily: if s exists then $s = t$

Sentences (a)–(c) say different things. Sentence (a) ascribes an essential property to the *objects* (or object) s and t: it says of them that they are necessarily identical if identical at all. If this really is a property of s and t then it is a property of s and t however named or described. If it is true of George Orwell and Eric Blair that necessarily they are one and the same then it is true of (the thing that is) the author of *Nineteen Eighty-Four* and (the thing that is) the author of *Animal Farm* that: necessarily, they are one and the same. Sentence (b) also describes an essential property of the object s but unlike (a) (which uses only pronouns after the necessity operator) its truth depends on what term t is used *inside* the scope of the necessity operator: even if George Orwell wrote *Animal Farm* it is *not* true that George Orwell has the property of being necessarily identical to the author of *Animal Farm*. Sentence (c) doesn't say anything about the *objects* s and t but rather that the *statement* $s = t$ is necessarily true. Its truth therefore depends on *both* terms s and t: even if the author of *Nineteen Eighty-Four* wrote *Animal Farm* it is not true that necessarily, the author of the first is the author of the second.

Similar distinctions must be observed regarding the necessity of distinctness. Of the following three sentences:

(d) If $s \neq t$ then s and t are such that necessarily: if either exists then they are not identical

(e) If $s \neq t$ then s is such that necessarily: if it exists then it is not identical to t

(f) If $s \neq t$ then necessarily: if s exists then it is not identical to t

– only (d) and (e) can be said to ascribe essential properties to *objects*: (f) concerns the modal status of a *statement* of distinctness and is therefore sensitive to what terms s and t appear after 'necessarily'.

When Kripke speaks of the necessity of identity and that of distinctness he normally means (c) and (f); he occasionally means (a) and (d). He never means (b) or (e) so we shall no longer consider them. It is usually quite clear what is meant. Kripke's claim is that (a) and (d) are true unrestrictedly; and that (c) and (f) are true if both s and t are rigid designators. As the arguments for the claims about identity and those about distinctness are quite symmetric there will be no harm in focusing only on the former, i.e. (a) and (c).

Kripke states in the preface to NN2 that the truth of (a) had been clear to him from the early sixties. This was for the following reason (here we use the standard terminology '$\square$' for 'it is necessary that:' and Russell's term '(x)' for 'for every x:'):

> Waiving fussy considerations deriving from the fact that x need not have necessary existence, it was clear from $(x)\square(x = x)$ and Leibnitz's Law that ... $(x)(y)(x = y \supset \square(x = y)$. (What pairs (x, y) could be counterexamples? Not pairs of distinct objects, for then the antecedent is false; nor any pair of an object and itself, for then the consequent is true.) (NN2:3; cf. IN:163)

Leibnitz's Law (the 'indiscernibility of identicals' or better the 'distinctness of discernibles') says that for any objects x and y, if $x = y$ then x and y have exactly the same properties: i.e. the truth of every substitution for F in $(x)(y)((x = y \& Fx) \supset Fy)$ – see NN2:3n4. The argument is then that since any x has the property of being necessarily identical to x, any object that *is* x must also have that property. In short: any thing is necessarily identical to itself.

It is plain that claim (a) follows from the conclusion of this argument. If *any* objects that are identical must be identical then this holds in particular for any objects that are identical to s and t. So we have $(x)(y)((x=s \;\&\; y=t \;\&\; s=t) \supset \Box(x=y))$, which is equivalent to (a) on the plausible assumption that the pronouns in (a) can be rendered as variables x and y. Nor does it make any difference if we reintroduce 'fussy considerations concerning necessary existence': the validity of the argument is unaffected if we substitute '$\Box$(if x exists then $x=x$)' and '$\Box$(if x exists then $x=y$)' for '$\Box(x=x)$' and '$\Box(x=y)$' respectively.

Is the argument compelling? It may of course be questioned whether $(x)\Box(x=x)$ makes sense on the Quinean grounds considered at 3.1.1. As I said, we are waiving these objections for present purposes. Always assuming that it *does* make sense, the argument appears to be flawless. Certainly there is no gainsaying Leibnitz's Law. It is hard to deny, given that x and y are the *same* thing, that they share all their properties. So the argument is sound.

Assuming that (a) isn't only true but true at all possible worlds we can easily establish (d). If at some possible world w the actually distinct objects x and y are identical then they are necessarily identical there and so identical at @, contrary to the supposition that they were actually distinct.

Kripke also claims that (c) is true *provided* that the *terms* referring to s and t (here 's' and 't') are rigid designators (NN2:3;NN:306/NN2:102). His argument is somewhat obscurely phrased and makes no allowances for the different kinds of rigidity (2.2.2). But we may easily reconstruct it as follows:

(24) The term 's' is inflexible (Premise)
(25) The term 't' is mildly rigid (Premise)
(26) It is actually the case that $s=t$ (Supposition)
(27) 's exists' is true at w (Supposition)
(28) 's' denotes at w the thing that is in fact s (from 24, 27)
(29) 's' denotes at w the thing that is in fact t (from 26, 28)
(30) 's' denotes at w what 't' denotes at w (from 25, 29)
(31) '$s = t$' is true at w (from 30)
(32) 'If s exists then $s = t$' is true at w (from 31, discharging 27)
(33) Necessarily, if s exists then $s = t$ (from 32, arbitrariness of w)
(34) If $s = t$ then necessarily, if s exists then $s = t$

This is claim (c). We see that it follows from the assumptions that s is inflexible and that t is mildly rigid. Intuitively the argument is very simple: if two terms are rigid then they refer to the same thing at all possible worlds: hence if they actually refer to the same things as one another then they do so at all possible worlds. But the argument as given illustrates just what kinds of rigidity we need to assume.

Exactly parallel arguments can be used to establish the necessity of distinctness.

Note that claims (a) and (c) are pure theses of philosophical logic: they need not be understood as saying anything about terms of English (NN2:4). But Kripke makes the further claim that statements involving proper names of English are necessarily true if true at all: if George Orwell = Eric Blair then necessarily, if George Orwell exists then he is Eric Blair. This claim follows from the argument just given *if* we can show that 'George Orwell' is inflexible and 'Eric Blair' is mildly rigid.

Can we show this? We have already seen (at 2.2.5) Kripke's test for mild rigidity: a term t is mildly rigid iff 'The thing that is in fact t might have both existed and failed to be t' is intuitively false. What about inflexibility? Kripke offers what is in effect a test for that as well: a term t is inflexible iff 'something other than what is in fact t might have been t' is intuitively false (NN:270/NN2:48).[5] Clearly 'Eric Blair' passes the first test: the thing that is in fact Eric Blair could not have both existed and failed to be Eric Blair. And 'George Orwell' passes the second test: nobody other than George Orwell could have been George Orwell. So we have established the premises of the argument for necessity of identity; the conclusion (34) therefore follows. The same argument will go through for any pair of English names. And the same goes for distinctness: if Mr Disraeli is distinct from Mr Gladstone then necessarily, if Mr Disraeli exists then he isn't Mr Gladstone.

But note finally that if *this* is how we are going to establish that 'George Orwell' is inflexible and 'Eric Blair' is mildly rigid then the argument for the necessity of identities involving natural language terms does *not* rely on rigidity at all, contrary to what is sometimes claimed (e.g. Gomez-Torrente 2006: 227–8). We can instead argue directly from the intuitions underpinning the rigidity claims, as follows:

(35) Nobody other than the thing that is in fact George Orwell could have been George Orwell (Premise)

(36) The thing that is in fact Eric Blair could not have both existed and failed to be Eric Blair (Premise)

(37) George Orwell exists at w (Supposition)

(38) George Orwell = Eric Blair (Supposition)

(39) The thing that is in fact George Orwell is George Orwell at w (from 35, 37)

(40) The thing that is in fact Eric Blair is George Orwell at w (38, 39)

(41) Eric Blair is George Orwell at w (36, 40)

(42) If George Orwell exists at w then he is Eric Blair there (41, discharging 37)

(43) Necessarily, if George Orwell exists then he is Eric Blair (42, arbitrariness of w)

(44) If George Orwell = Eric Blair then necessarily, if George Orwell exists then he is Eric Blair (43, discharging 38)

This argument doesn't mention rigidity at all. The same can therefore be said about the necessity of identity as was said about the second premise of the modal argument: it does *not* require any rigidity thesis. Such theses are rather side-effects of the premises on which it really relies.

More important than that is the conclusion that Kripke's arguments for all of (a), (c), (d) and (f) are decisive.

3.1.6 Conclusion
Kripke makes the following claims about essential properties of individuals.

(i)   That it makes sense to distinguish accidental from essential properties of individuals however described

(ii) That his ancestry is essential to a human being

(iii) That its material origin is essential to an artefact

(iv) That its original constitution is essential to a physical object

(v)   That identical/distinct objects are necessarily so

(vi) That statements of identity/distinctness involving rigid designators are necessary if true

I argued at 3.1.1 that the Kripke fails to motivate (i); at 3.1.2 that his arguments for (ii) either involve questionable intuitions or prove too much; at 3.1.3 that his argument for (iii) is invalid or involves an equally questionable premise; at 3.1.4 that the arguments for (iv) are invalid or questionable on the same grounds as those for (ii). I argued at 3.1.5 that we should sharply distinguish (v) and (vi) and (provided always that (i) is in fact true) that Kripke gives compelling grounds for both of them.

3.2 *A PRIORI* AND ESSENTIAL PROPERTIES OF NATURAL KINDS

Kripke argues (NN:314–9/NN2:116–23) that natural kinds do *not* have their superficial properties *a priori*: it isn't *a priori* that gold is yellow or that tigers are striped. He also argues (NN:319–21/NN2:123–6) that natural kinds have certain properties essentially: for example gold necessarily has the property of being an element with atomic number 79; water is necessarily H_2O. From these claims he infers (NN:322–3/NN2:127–8) that his rejection of FRTC for proper names applies also to natural kind terms. Finally he argues (NN:323–7/NN2:128–34) that identifications involving natural kind terms (e.g. 'Light is a stream of photons') are if true at all necessarily so.

But what *is* a natural kind? And what is a natural kind term? Kripke doesn't say very much about this. All you need to know is that natural kinds include elements and compounds like gold and water and animal and vegetable species like tigers and elm trees. And natural kind *terms* are the standard expressions that are used by scientists or ordinary speakers to classify these substances or species (e.g. 'gold', 'water', 'tiger', 'elm').

3.2.1 A Priori *Properties of Natural Kinds*
By 'phenomenal properties' of a natural kind I mean those by which we ordinarily identify its instances. The phenomenal properties of water include potability, transparency and being liquid at room temperature. The phenomenal properties of gold include heaviness, yellowness and malleability. The phenomenal properties of tigers include four-leggedness, carnivorousness and felinity (looking like a big striped cat). Kripke makes three claims about phenomenal properties: (i) no single phenomenal property applies *a priori* to any natural kind; (ii) it is not *a priori* that something possessing *all* the

phenomenal properties of a natural kind belongs to that natural kind; (iii) it is not *a priori* that *any* of its phenomenal properties applies to a natural kind.

(i) Consider the natural kind *gold* and its phenomenal property of yellowness. Kripke argues that it isn't *a priori* that gold is yellow: certain experiences would lead us to judge that it is not:

> Could we discover that gold was not in fact yellow? ... Suppose there were an optical illusion which made the substance appear to be yellow; but, in fact, once the peculiar properties of the atmosphere were removed, we would see that it is actually blue ... Would there on this basis be an announcement in the newspapers: 'It has turned out that there is no gold. Gold does not exist. What we took to be gold is not in fact gold.'? ... It seems to me that there would be no such announcement. On the contrary, what would be announced would be that though it appeared that gold was yellow, in fact gold has turned out not to be yellow, but blue. (NN:315–6/NN2:118)

Some possible future course of experience might prompt us to judge that gold isn't after all yellow; hence it isn't *a priori* that gold is yellow. It is easy to imagine a similar argument to show that gold isn't *a priori* heavy; and it is possible though somewhat harder to imagine one that shows gold not to be *a priori* malleable.

These arguments are persuasive. We *might* make the discovery that Kripke mentions (though it is unlikely): if we did, it is highly plausible that we should not conclude that gold doesn't exist but only that it isn't yellow.

(ii) Kripke also argues that there could for all we know be things that possess all the phenomenal properties of some natural kind without being an instance of it. Not only *could* there be such a thing: there *is* such a thing – iron sulphide (iron pyrites) or 'fool's gold'. Fool's gold possesses all the properties by which we *ordinarily* identify gold (it is heavy, malleable and yellow) but it isn't gold (NN:316/NN2:119). Again this is plausible.

However it is unclear that the point applies to biological kinds like tigers. If we discovered that some of the animals that we call 'tigers' looked and behaved for all the world like the other tigers but in fact had a distinct genetic make-up, what should we say? Should we say that these are after all *not* tigers or that there are *two kinds* of tiger? 'Say what you like as long as you know all the facts' – but my own intuition is that in that case there would be two kinds of tigers.

In short: Kripke's claim was that it isn't *a priori* that anything possessing all the phenomenal properties of a kind belongs to that kind. While this is intuitively plausible for certain chemical kinds it is perhaps less so for biological kinds like tigers.

(iii) Kripke argues finally that it isn't *a priori* that an instance of a natural kind possesses *any* of the properties by which we ordinarily identify it. The example in this case is tigers:

> Just as something may have all the properties by which we ori-ginally identified tigers and yet not be a tiger, so we might also find out tigers had *none* of the properties by which we originally identified them. Perhaps *none* are quadrupedal, none tawny yellow, none carnivorous, and so on; all these properties turn out to be based on optical illusions or other errors, as in the case of gold. (NN:318/NN2:121)

The idea is presumably that we might discover that some sort of illusion is prevalent in tiger-infested areas; it might further turn out that really tigers are small, and blue, and have no legs at all. Al-though this is highly unlikely we can hardly rule out *a priori* that such an illusion exists. And it is plausible – in so far as it is possible to judge at all – that were we to discover that illusion the natural response would be, not that tigers did not after all exist, but that *tigers* were in fact small, blue and legless rather than large, tawny and quadrupedal. Similar plausibility attaches to the corresponding claim about gold.

In short: Kripke claims that it isn't *a priori* that all members of a kind possess *any* of the phenomenal properties associated with it. And this is probably true.

3.2.2 Essential Properties of Natural Kinds

Kripke also holds that there are properties of natural kinds that empirical investigation could reveal but which apply to them of metaphysical necessity. An example is the property of gold that it has atomic number 79: every atom of gold has 79 protons in its nucleus. Certainly this is a property of gold. But is it a *necessary* or a *contingent* property of it?

This question must be carefully distinguished from a related question to do with properties of *individuals*. It might be asked of a given gold object: could *it* have both existed and failed to be made of material with atomic number 79? This isn't the question that presently concerns us. What concerns us is not whether anything that is golden has its atomic number essentially but whether *gold* has its atomic number essentially (W:116).

Kripke argues as follows that it does:

> Consider a counterfactual situation in which, let us say, fool's gold or iron pyrites was actually found in various mountains in the United States, or in areas of South Africa and the Soviet Union. Suppose that all the areas which actually contain gold now, contained pyrites instead ... Would we say, of this counterfactual situation, that in that situation gold would not even have been an element (because pyrites would not have been an element)? It seems to me that we would not. We would instead describe this as a situation in which a substance, say iron pyrites, which is not gold, would have been found in the very mountains which actually contain gold and would have had the very properties by which we commonly identify gold. But it would not be gold; it would be something else. (NN:320/NN2:124–5)[6]

Similar arguments will show e.g. that cats are necessarily animals if they are animals at all (NN:321/NN2:125–6); and presumably also that a biological kind necessarily has whatever genetic make-up scientific enquiry tells us is common to all of its instances.

But does this argument really show that gold must have had atomic number 79 (or even the weaker claim that gold could not have failed to be an element)? If that is what the argument is supposed to show then it must be proceeding in some such manner as this. There is a possible world w where iron pyrites (or some other gold counterfeit[7]) is found instead of gold in all the mines etc. where gold is actually found. But then:

(1) If it is metaphysically possible that gold does not have atomic number 79 then it does not have atomic number 79 at w (Premise)

(2) But gold *does* have atomic number 79 at w: the material found in mines etc. at w is *not* gold (Premise)

(3)   Hence it is not metaphysically possible that gold does not have atomic number 79 (from 1, 2)

Plainly the argument is valid. But there is one obvious reason for doubting premise (1). Kripke describes *w* as a world where 'all areas which actually contain gold now, contained pyrites *instead*' (my emphasis). So he has built into the very description of *w* that what is found in those areas is iron pyrites *and not gold*. It is trivial that in *that* world iron pyrites both exists and isn't gold: but could there not be a world at which gold both existed and *was* iron pyrites? We can easily amend the argument to get around this objection. We simply suppose that *w* contains iron pyrites where gold is actually found while making no *stipulation* that the iron pyrites is not gold.

Turning to premise (2), we see that Kripke bases it on intuition. But the same problems arise here as arose in connection with his earlier appeals to intuition. First: the intuition behind (2) is easily disrupted if we choose to describe *w* in a slightly different way. Suppose I describe it as a world where all the stuff that plays the actual role of gold has the chemical structure actually possessed by iron pyrites (and nothing has the actual chemical structure of gold), and then say to the layman: would that have been a world where gold was a compound or one where gold did not exist? I can think of three responses: they *all* feel intuitively acceptable; and (c) is perhaps the most natural:

(a)   It would be a world where gold did not have atomic number 79
(b)   It would be a world where gold did not exist
(c)   You could call it either: it doesn't really matter so long as you are consistent about it

In light of this it is no use simply appealing to intuitions. Kripke needs to give an argument for preferring (b) to either (a) or (c).

The first problem with the intuition behind (2) was that (b) isn't clearly the right thing to say. The second problem with the intuition behind (2) is that we can imagine circumstances where (b) is clearly the *wrong* thing to say. I might say:

(d)   If gold had been a compound (and so had not had atomic number 79) then it would have been more difficult to extract

I don't know whether (d) is true. But it certainly makes intuitive sense even if we are certain that in fact gold is an element. And that presupposes the metaphysical possibility that gold was *not* an element. Now Kripke *might* respond that (d) ought to be analysed as being, not really about *gold* at all, but rather as being about whatever has the phenomenal properties of gold. But what reasons are there for rejecting the intuition that (d) is about gold other than its clash with another intuition – that (b) is *the* correct way to describe this possibility? The correct conclusion to draw is that we have contrary intuitions about metaphysical possibility and therefore that these intuitions cannot always be trusted. To say instead that we should hold on to (b) and regard (d) as meaningless or trivial appears arbitrary.

In short: Kripke argues that elements like gold have their atomic number (and their elementhood) necessarily. But as I have construed his argument, one of its premises rests on a highly questionable intuition. I am not at all sure that no reply is available: but at any rate Kripke himself says nothing to address this question.

3.2.3 Semantic Consequences of These Claims

After giving the arguments described at 3.2.1 and 3.2.2 Kripke says:

> According to the view I advocate, then, terms for natural kinds are much closer to proper names than is ordinarily supposed. The old term 'common name' is thus quite appropriate for predicates marking out species or natural kinds, such as 'cow' or 'tiger'. My considerations apply also, however, to certain mass terms for natural kinds, such as 'gold', 'water' and the like ... Certainly 'cow' and 'tiger' are *not* short for the conjunction of properties a dictionary would take to define them, as Mill thought. (NN:322/NN2:127–8)

Here Kripke is denying the Frege-Russell Thesis for predicates like 'gold', 'tiger' etc.: the thesis that the *meaning* of these terms is given by some non-trivial set of properties.

What are his grounds for this? He acknowledges that they are implicit (NN:327/NN2:134) so we shall have to reconstruct his argument. The simplest reconstruction is that the arguments considered at 3.2.2 and 3.2.1 respectively support modal and epistemic arguments against the Frege-Russell Thesis for predicates. Let us consider these in turn.

(A) *The Modal Argument*. We saw reasons for doubting Kripke's view that gold is essentially an element with atomic number 79. But supposing that he is right about this, can we infer anything about the meaning of the term 'gold'? Here is an argument:

(4) If 'Gold' means the same as 'The stuff that has such-and-such phenomenal properties' then it is necessarily the case that anything with those properties is gold (Premise)

(5) It is not necessarily the case that anything with those properties is gold (Premise)

(6) If FRT as applied to *predicates* is true then 'Gold' means the same as 'The stuff that has such-and-such phenomenal properties' (Premise)

(7) 'Gold' does not mean the same as 'The stuff that has such-and-such phenomenal properties' (from 4, 5)

(8) FRT as applied to predicates is false (from 6, 7)

Now if the Kripkean argument considered at 3.2.2 is correct then we know that gold necessarily has the property of being an element with atomic number 79. And we have also seen that something might *not* have that atomic number and yet have the phenomenal properties of gold, including its location in certain mines (in the example we imagined that iron sulphide had those properties). Therefore if the argument considered at 3.2.2 is correct then there might have been material that was *not* gold and yet had all the phenomenal properties of gold. That argument is therefore grounds for premise (5). The argument is valid: so what about premises (4) and (6)?

Unfortunately there are grounds for doubting both premises: these are essentially the same as the objections to premises (1) and (3) of the modal argument against FRT (2.2.3). The objection to premise (4) (cf. 2.2.4) is that we have not been given any notion of synonymy that makes it plausible: why should two predicates not have the same 'meaning' in *some* sense and yet behave differently in modal contexts? And the objection to premise (6) (cf. 2.2.6) is that FRT as applied to predicates can (while retaining fealty to its supposed motivations – see 2.1.2) be modified to state that 'Gold' means the same as 'The stuff that actually has such-and-such phenomenal properties': and in that case the present argument is impotent to disturb it.

In short: I cannot see that any modal argument about natural kind terms can evade the objections to the argument about proper names. Clearly Kripke would not agree, since he doesn't find those objections compelling. Still, he strongly hints that it is not any *modal* argument that he regards as the primary objection to the Frege-Russell Thesis as applied to predicates (NN:322–3/NN2:128). The weight of his arguments against that thesis must therefore derive from the epistemological argument.

(B) *The Epistemological Argument.* We saw at 3.2.1 that Kripke argued for three claims: (i) no single phenomenal property applies *a priori* to a natural kind; (ii) it isn't *a priori* that something possessing *all* the phenomenal properties of a natural kind belongs to that natural kind; (iii) it isn't *a priori* that *any* of its phenomenal properties applies to a natural kind. Now (iii) entails (i); so if (i) defeats the Frege-Russell Thesis for predicates then so does (iii). Moreover if none of (i)–(iii) by itself defeats that thesis I cannot see how they can defeat it together. I therefore consider only claims (ii) and (iii) separately, asking of each whether it defeats the Frege-Russell Thesis.

One might argue from (ii) as follows:

(9) If FRT as applied to predicates is true then it is *a priori* that anything possessing *all* the phenomenal properties associated with gold will itself be gold (Premise)

(10) It is not *a priori* that anything possessing all those phenomenal properties is gold (Premise)

(11) Therefore FRT as applied to predicates is false (from 9, 10)

Claim (ii) provides grounds for premise (10); and the argument is valid. But is premise (9) true?

By 'the phenomenal properties of gold' we meant this: the features by which we ordinarily identify a thing as an instance of gold. But one might argue without prejudice to FRT that we associate a *further* feature with the term 'gold': namely the fact that it forms a *kind*; that is, a substance with some distinctive microstructure that is causally responsible for its phenomenal properties.

There are two ways to misunderstand this. The first is to read it as follows: according to FRT, 'gold' applies *a priori* to anything that *has* such-and-such phenomenal features *and* is itself a kind, i.e. has some microstructure that is responsible for its phenomenal features. That claim is vulnerable to the same counterexample: since iron sulphide *is* itself a kind in this sense and since it *does* have the phenomenal properties of gold it will follow from this misreading that if FRT is true then 'gold' applies to iron sulphide. So misunderstood, the amendment is of no help.

The second misreading is this: according to FRT it is part of the *meaning* of 'gold' that it denotes an element with atomic number 79. If this were true then premise (9) of the argument would be false. FRT would not imply that it was *a priori* that anything possessing all the *phenomenal* properties of gold (but not its microstructural ones) counts as gold. But FRT would still be false: for it is *not* part of the meaning of 'gold' that 'gold has atomic number 79' expresses a truth. Someone who fails to realize this suffers not from misunderstanding but only from ignorance.

The way I intended the claim was this: it is part of the meaning of 'gold' that if *two* items are samples of gold then they will have the *same* microstructural features (whatever these in fact are). This position is occluded if one thinks that according to FRT, the only information about gold that can contribute to the meaning of 'gold' concerns features by which we identify a *single* thing as an instance of it. But nothing in the motivation for the Frege-Russell Thesis commits it to that. A defender of FRT may therefore say that, as well as associating with 'gold' the description 'has such-and-such phenomenal properties', competent users of that term are also prepared *not* to apply 'gold' to two items with differing microstructures (cf. Dummett 1963: 193–4). Of course one may regard it as *a priori* true that no two items that so differ are both gold even if one doesn't know *a priori* (or at all) what the actual microstructure of gold *is*.

A defender of FRT for predicates who takes that line will of course not be committed either to (9) or to its consequence that 'gold' refers to iron sulphide. For iron sulphide doesn't have atomic number 79; on this view it therefore follows (and it is *a priori* that it follows) that stuff with atomic number 79 and iron sulphide cannot *both* be gold. So the argument based on claim (ii) is unsound.

The other epistemological argument proceeded from claim (iii) that it isn't *a priori* that *any* of its phenomenal properties applies to a natural kind. The argument would presumably run as follows:

(12) If FRT as applied to predicates is true then it is *a priori* that nothing lacking *all* of the phenomenal properties associated with tigers will itself be a tiger (Premise)

(13) It is not *a priori* that nothing lacking all those phenomenal properties is a tiger (Premise)

(14) Therefore FRT as applied to predicates is false (from 12, 13)

Here claim (iii) functions as the grounds for premise (13). But now it is unclear that premise (12) is true, for similar reasons to those raised at 2.4.2. It might indeed turn out that we were all along deluded about *all* the phenomenal properties of tigers: it turns out that tigers are not after all fierce, large and tawny; they are in fact docile, small and blue. But why should we say in that case (as we probably would) that we had all along held delusional beliefs *about tigers* rather than that there *are* none? Isn't the reason this: part of the 'cluster' that we associated with 'tiger' was something like 'biological kind predominantly responsible for our (or experts') use of "tiger"'? But in that case (12) is false. Just so long as this component of the cluster has sufficient weight in suitable contexts the defender of FRT can maintain the following: for all we know *a priori*, the causal source of our talk about tigers might have *none* of the phenomenal features associated with tigers; hence for all we know *a priori*, *tigers* might have none of those features. Hence the epistemological argument based on premise (iii) is unsound.

In conclusion: even if we accept Kripke's epistemological and modal claims regarding natural kinds, it is unclear what follows about natural kind terms. In particular it is unclear that the epistemological and modal claims refute the Frege-Russell Thesis for natural kind terms.

3.2.4 Theoretical Identifications

The discussion at NN:323–7/NN2:128–34 concerns 'theoretical identifications': statements representing scientific discoveries about what a natural kind or phenomenon *is*. For example: light is a stream of photons; lightning is a form of electrical discharge; heat is a form of molecular motion; gravity is a form of curvature. There are also examples involving chemical and biological as well as physical kinds: water is H_2O; tigers are animals. Kripke argues that these statements are true necessarily if at all. There could not possibly have been light rays that were not streams of photons;

there could not possibly have been heat that wasn't molecular motion.

The first argument for this follows a by now familiar pattern:

> It seems to me that any case which someone will think of, which he thinks at first is a case in which heat – contrary to what is actually the case – would have been something other than molecular motion, would actually be a case in which some creatures with different nerve endings from ours inhabit this planet? ... and in which these creatures were sensitive to that something else, say light, in such a way that they felt the same thing that we feel when we feel heat. But this is not a situation in which, say, light would have been heat, or even in which a stream of photons would have been heat, but a situation in which a stream of photons would have produced the characteristic sensations which *we* call 'sensations of heat'. (NN:325/NN2:131–2)

When we try to imagine a possible world where heat is *not* molecular motion, the best we can do is to imagine a world where what *feels like* heat is not molecular motion. We can certainly imagine *that*; but that isn't yet imagining that *heat* isn't molecular motion. Instead one is only imagining that something that *is not* heat *feels* as though it is. Similarly, when one thinks one is imagining that water isn't H_2O or that light isn't a stream of photons one is really not imagining that. One is only imagining this: that there is stuff that *looks* like and *tastes* like but *is not* water; or that there is stuff that *looks like* but *is not* light.

Does this show that heat *could not* have been anything other than molecular motion? I won't state in detail the reasons for doubting this argument because they are parallel to those raised at 3.1.2 against the essentiality of human ancestry. Put very briefly: (i) It often seems arbitrary whether we say that heat is not molecular motion at some possible world or rather that something else feels like heat there. (ii) It is a very natural and possibly true thing to say e.g. 'If heat had been a form of electromagnetic radiation (and not molecular motion) then it would have tended to propagate more quickly'.

However Kripke does appear (and is frequently taken: see e.g. Hanna 1998) to have *another* argument for the necessity of theoretical identifications. This is visible in the following:

[W]e've discovered eventually that [heat] is in fact molecular motion. When we have discovered this, we've discovered an identification which gives us an essential property of this phenomenon. We have discovered a phenomenon which in all possible worlds will be molecular motion – which could not have failed to be molecular motion because that's what the phenomenon *is*. (NN:326/NN2:133)

The phenomenon of heat 'could not have failed to be molecular motion because that's what the phenomenon *is*'. Kripke *may* be appealing here to an argument from *identity* to necessity of the sort already considered at 3.1.5 (for further evidence that this was his intention see NN:331/NN2:140). Could such an argument show that heat is necessarily molecular motion?

The argument would be along the lines of the argument from (24) to (34) at 3.1.5. A full statement of it would therefore have to settle whether 'heat' was persistently rigid, obstinately rigid or whatever. Ignoring those issues here (since they will make little difference) we may sketch the argument as follows:

(15) 'Heat' and 'Molecular Motion' are rigid designators (Premise)
(16) 'Heat = Molecular Motion' is true (Premise)
(17) 'Heat' refers to the same thing at all possible worlds (from 15)
(18) 'Molecular Motion' refers to the same thing at all possible worlds (from 15)
(19) 'Heat' and 'Molecular Motion' refer to the same thing *as one another* at all possible worlds (from 16, 17, 18)
(20) 'Heat = Molecular Motion' is necessarily true (from 19)

But there are two difficulties with this argument. First: it will only ever show *identity statements* discovered by empirical enquiry to be necessary: the inference from (16), (17) and (18) to (19) requires that the relation between heat and molecular motion described at (16) be strict identity. So the argument won't work for other theoretical statements such as 'cats are animals' or 'gold is an element': we cannot say that *these* are identity statements.

More seriously, the notion of 'rigid designator' doesn't extend straightforwardly to natural kind terms. To say that a name designates rigidly is to say that it refers to the same thing at any possible world. But if we define rigidity for natural kind terms in this way then we face the question: what *do* natural kind terms like 'gold' and 'heat' refer to?

One might say that 'heat' refers at any world to the set of things that are hot at that world. But then premise (15) is false: the set of hot things varies from one world to another and so 'heat' (or 'gold') isn't rigid. One might alternatively say that 'heat' or 'gold' refers to a *property* or *kind*: the same property or kind at every world (Donnellan 1983). In that case premise (15) is true but now premise (16) is unreasonable, for it isn't clear how empirical science can tell us that 'heat' and 'molecular motion' denote the *same* properties. It can of course tell us that the properties are *co-extensive*: something is hot if and only if its molecules are in motion (or the relational version of this: NN:330/NN2:138). But plenty of distinct properties are co-extensive, e.g. the property of being a coin in my pocket and that of being a silver coin in my pocket; or arguably those of tri-laterality and triangularity. So on either view of what 'heat' refers to the argument is unsound.

One might alternatively propose the following. A predicate like 'is heat' or 'is gold' is rigid if and only if: for any object *x* that it *applies* to, it applies to *x* at all possible worlds. Thus 'gold' is rigid because, roughly, anything that *is* gold could not have failed to be gold; similarly any instance of molecular motion could not have been anything other than an instance of molecular motion (for more detail see Gomez-Torrente 2006). However, even if 'heat' and 'molecular motion' *are* rigid in *this* sense, we can only deduce the following:

(a) Nothing that *actually* exists and is heat could both have *been* heat and *failed* to be molecular motion

(Soames 2002: 257). This however falls short of the necessity of theoretical identification advertised at the start of this section: the claim that

(b) There could not have *been* instances of heat that were not instances of molecular motion

It is easy to see that (b) doesn't follow from (a) if we reflect that (b) but not (a) rules out the possibility that actually non-existent in-stances of heat both exist and fail to be molecular motion.

Moreover, the *interest* of Kripke's claim about theoretical identifications lies in its supposedly damaging consequences for materialistic identifications of mental and physical states or events (e.g. pain and neural stimulation). I shall argue at 3.4.8 that even if something of the form of (b) *does* have these damaging consequences for materialism, something of the form of (a) certainly doesn't. So the fact that (a) but not (b) can be derived from this novel interpretation of rigidity would hardly commend the latter to Kripke.

I conclude that no convincing arguments have been given for the necessity of theoretical identifications. We saw two arguments: one of them was parallel to the argument concerning human ancestry and the other was parallel to the argument concerning individual identity. The first argument is little more than an invitation to 'intuit' its conclusion. The second argument leaves open how rigidity is supposed to apply to natural kind terms. And we saw no answer to that question that gives us satisfaction.

3.2.5 Conclusion
We saw that Kripke argues:

(i)   That its associated phenomenal properties are neither *a priori* necessary nor sufficient for membership of a natural kind
(ii) That natural kinds have certain properties essentially
(iii) That from (i) and maybe (ii) it follows that his anti-descriptivism with regard to proper names applies also to natural kind terms
(iv) That identifications involving natural kind terms are if true at all necessarily so

His arguments for (i) are persuasive but his arguments for (ii), (iii) and (iv) are not.

3.3 MODAL ILLUSION

Kripke thinks the following statements are necessary if true: that Elizabeth II is the daughter of George VI (essentiality of human ancestry); that this desk was made from that piece of wood (essentiality of material origin); that this desk was originally constituted of wood (essentiality of original constitution); that George

Orwell is Eric Blair (necessity of identity for individuals); that gold is an element (necessity of kindhood for natural kinds); and that light is a stream of photons (necessity of theoretical identifications).

But all of these claims are *a posteriori*: we can imagine experience leading us to reject any of them. Indeed Kripke himself accepts that it *could have turned out* that gold wasn't an element or that light wasn't a stream of photons (NN:331/NN2:140–1). How then can it be *necessary* that light is a stream of photons? The tension arises from the fact that Kripke's examples violate the traditional identification of the *a priori* and the necessary (a classic statement is Kant 1929: B3–4). It seems that a necessary truth *must* be knowable *a priori*, i.e. experience could *not* have shown it to be false: since the true statement that Elizabeth II is the daughter of George VI cannot be known *a priori* it must therefore be contingent.

In order to grasp the nature and the importance of Kripke's response we need to grasp the following two things. Firstly: he grants that in *some* sense gold might have turned out not to have been an element etc. We need to be clear about what this sense is. Secondly: he thinks that the intuition that gold could have turned out not to be an element in *this* sense gives rise to the illusion that gold might not have *been* an element. We need to be clear as to whether this is true.

3.3.1 'It Could Have Turned Out ...'
What do we mean when we say that this (originally wooden) table might have turned out to have been made of ice? Kripke says that this phrase can be interpreted in two ways: on the first interpretation it implies that the table might not have *been* made of ice and is itself neither true nor a consequence of the fact that the discovery that it was wooden is *a posteriori*. On the second interpretation it does *not* imply that the table might have been made of ice and is a true consequence of the *a posteriori* status of the discovery that it wasn't.

The first interpretation is this: 'this table could have turned out to have been made of ice' means: there is a possible world where we know that this table *was* made of ice. On this interpretation:

> The objector is correct when he argues that if I hold that this table could not have been made of ice, then I must also hold that it could not have turned out to be made of ice; *it could have*

turned out that P entails that *P* could have been the case. (NN:332/NN2:141–2)

Clearly on this interpretation 'the table could have turned out to be made of ice' is incompatible with Kripke's claim that it is essentially wooden. So he must say that in this sense the table could *not* have turned out to have been made of ice. But isn't it true that if we can only know *a posteriori* that the table was made of wood and not ice then it *could* in this sense have turned out to be made of ice?

Kripke says not. All that follows is that the table could have been made of ice in the *second* sense of that expression. He explains this as follows:

> What, then, does the intuition that the table might have turned out to have been made of ice or of anything else, that it might even have turned out not to be made of molecules, amount to? I think that it means simply that there might have been *a table* looking and feeling just like this one and placed in this very position in the room, which was in fact made of ice. In other words, I (or some conscious being) could have been *qualitatively in the same epistemic situation* that in fact obtains, I could have the same sensory evidence that I in fact have, about *a table* which was made of ice. (NN:332/NN2:142)

Clearly if this is what 'the table might have turned out to have been made of ice' means, then the statement is both true and not in conflict with the thesis that *this* table could *not* have been made of ice. All it shows is that there is some possible world where we (or creatures relevantly like us) have the same sensory evidence as we actually do but in which the thing that looks like 'our' table is in fact *another* table that happens to be made of ice. And that is all we mean when we say that we can only know *a posteriori* that the table is made of wood and not ice.

The same interpretation of 'It could have turned out that . . .' will defuse arguments against the necessity of other *a posteriori* statements. If it is claimed that light could have turned out not to be a stream of photons, Kripke will reply that this only establishes the following: that there is some possible world where *a* phenomenon A is identified in the same way as we identify light, and that phenomenon is in fact not a stream of photons. But A would not *be* light; nor therefore does it follow that *light* might not have been a stream of photons.

In fact the strategy implicit in Kripke's statement is insufficiently general if the term 'sensory' is doing any work there at all. There are necessary *a posteriori* truths concerning objects of which we have no sensory evidence and which could yet have turned out in the second sense to be false. Suppose that we dub the author of Genesis 'J' and the author of Exodus 'K'; and suppose we discover that J = K. This is a necessary truth, and yet it could intuitively have turned out that J and K were distinct. But (i) *It could have turned out that J and K were distinct* cannot mean (ii) *There might have been somebody who looked like J and yet was not K*: this follows from the fact that (ii) but not (i) is a trivial consequence of the fact that J had a twin who never wrote anything. There is none the less an interpretation of (i) that makes it both plausible and consistent with the necessity of J = K: (i) is true in the sense that *It might have been the case that the author of Genesis was distinct from K*. This suggests that the intuition expressed by 'It could have turned out that *X* wasn't *Y*' ought in general to be interpreted as follows: possibly, something both satisfies the *description by means of which we pick out the reference of 'X'* and is distinct from *Y*. This approach covers the 'table' and 'light' examples if the descriptions associated with 'this table' and 'light' include sensory ones; it also covers the present biblical example.

Kripke suggests that this generalization is acceptable to him in the last sentence of the following:

What was the strategy used above to handle the apparent contingency of certain cases of the necessary *a posteriori*? The strategy was to argue that although the statement is itself necessary, someone could, *qualitatively* speaking, be in the same epistemic situation as the original, and in such a situation a *qualitative* analogous statement could be false. In the case of identities between two rigid designators, the strategy can be approximated by a simpler one: Consider how the references of the designators are determined; if these coincide only contingently, it is this fact which gives the original statement its illusion of contingency. (NN:338/NN2:150)

But it is not clear why he describes the second strategy as either simpler than, or as an approximation to, the first. It is rather that the first strategy is a special case of the second. Moreover the second strategy applies to cases other than *identity* statements: it applies also to theoretical identifications. If A and B are both theoretical (i.e. not directly observable) physical phenomena (say, gravity and spatial curvature), then the theoretical identification of A and B is necessary: and yet in some sense they might have turned out distinct. This just means that there might have been a phenomenon whose reference was fixed in the way we fix that of 'gravity' but which failed to be the phenomenon of spatial curvature.

Having admitted this more general strategy we can also see that 'It might have turned out that X and Y were distinct' can mean *three* different things. Suppose we use the descriptions D1 and D2 to determine the references of 'X' and 'Y' respectively, and that in fact X and Y are the same person, or object, or phenomenon. Then 'It could have turned out that X and Y were distinct' is both true and compatible with the necessity of 'X is Y' if taken in *any* of the following three senses:

(a) There is a possible world where the thing that satisfies D1 is distinct from Y

(b) There is a possible world where the thing that satisfies D2 is distinct from X

(c) There is a possible world where the thing that satisfies D1 is distinct from the thing that satisfies D2

For example: someone who says truly that light might have turned out not to be a stream of photons might mean either (a) that at some possible world what affects our retinas in the way that light actually does is not a stream of photons; or (b) that at some possible world what impinges on our photon-detectors in the way that photons actually do is not light; or (c) that at some possible world what affects our retinas in the way light actually does, doesn't impinge on our photon-detectors in the way that photons actually do. These really are three different claims: neither of (a) and (b) entails the other; (c) entails the disjunction of (a) and (b) but doesn't entail either in particular; and the conjunction of (a) and (b) doesn't entail (c).[8]

However, there are cases where the intuition behind a claim of contingency cannot be rehabilitated in this way. Kripke holds that one might refer to an individual even though one is (and perhaps knows that one is) aware of *no* description that picks him out uniquely. He gives the following example:

> In fact, most people, when they think of Cicero, just think of *a famous Roman orator*, without any pretension to think either that there was only one famous Roman orator or that one must know something else about Cicero to have a referent for that name. (NN:291–2/NN2:81)

But suppose I am in this position with regard to 'Cicero' and 'Tully'. All I can say about either is that it refers to a famous Roman orator. Now suppose I believe that Cicero *is* Tully but that Cicero might have turned out *not* to be Tully. Kripke thinks it would be a mistake for me to infer that Cicero might not have *been* Tully: but then what does my intuition of contingency amount to? Kripke must reconstrue it in one of three ways:

(d) At some possible world the thing that satisfies the description associated with 'Cicero' is not Tully
(e) At some possible world the thing that satisfies the description associated with 'Tully' is not Cicero
(f) At some possible world the thing that satisfies the description associated with 'Cicero' is not the thing that satisfies the description associated with 'Tully'

But I have *no* description that picks out Cicero (or therefore Tully): so *none* of (d)–(f) is a plausible reading of 'Cicero might have turned out not to be Tully'. My only description associated with 'Cicero' is 'a famous Roman orator': so (d) just says that at some possible world Tully isn't a famous Roman orator. *That* I don't doubt: but it is hardly what I meant when I said that Cicero might have turned out distinct from Tully. The same point applies to (e). And as for (f), if it means anything true at all it can only mean that there might have been *two* famous Roman orators. But again that isn't what I meant when I said that Cicero might have turned out not to be Tully.

In short, if Kripke is correct to say that we can refer to things without *any* description available to pick them out uniquely, then the intuitions that *a posteriori* identities are contingent cannot always be reconstrued in the manner he recommends. The best response may be that when we use 'Cicero' to refer to Cicero we *do* always have some description in mind that picks him out (e.g. 'The person called "Cicero"'). In that case the objection to Kripke's account isn't that it is false but only that it is in conflict with other things he says.

In conclusion: Kripke says that the intuition that necessary *a posteriori* identifications 'X is Y' could have turned out false isn't in conflict with their necessity. We saw that the most plausible way to understand them is roughly as follows: that the *descriptions* by which we *determine the reference* of 'X' and 'Y' are only contingently satisfied by the same thing. Finally, we saw a case that this account appears impotent to handle.

3.3.2 The Illusion of Contingency
We have just seen a sense in which 'It could have turned out that X and Y were distinct' expresses a true intuition. Kripke thinks that that intuition is typically *misinterpreted* as an indication of the *contingency* of the identity or theoretical identification of X and Y. They give rise to judgements of *apparent* but not real contingency (NN:338/NN2:150).

But does that really amount to an explanation of the apparent contingency of *a posteriori* necessities? There is one reason for doubting this.

This is that the argument threatens to show that *all* apparent contingency is illusory. Even if this table couldn't have been made of ice Kripke *does* grant that it might e.g. have been transported to the Kremlin (NN:331–2/NN2:126). But suppose we said that the intuition that it might have been so transported is in fact an illusion: all we are really imagining is that

there might have been *a table* looking and feeling just like this one and placed in this very position in the room, which had in fact been transported to the Kremlin. In other words, I (or some conscious being) could have been *qualitatively in the same epistemic situation* that in fact obtains, I could have the same sensory evidence that I in fact have, about *a table* which was in fact once in the Kremlin.

In short: we have the following statements:

(a) When we think we imagine *this* table having been made of ice we are really only imagining that *a* table that looked like it was made of ice

(b) When we think that we imagine *this* table having been transported to the Kremlin we are really only imagining that *a* table that looked like it was transported there

Analyses of this sort might be called 'counterpart' analyses: facts about what might have happened to *this* table are really facts about what happens to *other* relevantly similar tables at other possible worlds (see NN:344–5n13/NN2:45n13). Now what principled reason is there for applying a counterpart analysis to 'this table might have turned out to be made from ice' but withholding it from 'this table might have been transported to the Kremlin'? In short, what reason is there for asserting (a) but denying (b)?

In two sentences Kripke gives two apparently distinct replies:

[a] applies only because we are *not* interested in what might have been true of *this particular table*, but in what might or might not be true of *a table* given certain evidence. It is precisely because it is *not* true that this table might have been made of ice from the Thames that we must turn here to qualitative descriptions and counterparts. (NN:333/NN2:142)

The first sentence appears to be saying this. When we talk about what the table might have turned out to have been made from we are *not* talking about what *this* table might have been made from. We are talking about a possible situation in which we have the same evidence but where *a* table that looked and felt like this one was in fact made from ice. The implicit line of thought *appears* to be that when you use 'it might have turned out that ...' to express the insecurity of your evidence as to the table's constitution, all you are saying is that there is an evidentially identical possible situation in which *a* table both appears to be just like the actual one and is in fact made from ice. When we are not interested in talking about the insecurity of our evidence but only in what *might* have *happened* to this table, we really are speaking about *this very* table.

The second sentence seems to be saying that the only reason that

(a) is true is that we already know that the table could *not* have been made of ice: it is precisely because that truth is contrary to our intuition of contingency that we must find some way of re-interpreting the intuition.

Let us deal with the first sentence first. If my interpretation is correct then there are reasons for doubting it. Consider the following fantasy scenario. There are highly sophisticated robots that are capable of thoughts and experiences, just like human beings. Their mental life can be manipulated by controlling their electrical inputs. Suppose that many robots have been fed with just the same thoughts and experiences as I have actually had: so the robots are in exactly the same evidential situation as I am. But *I* am not a robot; I am flesh and blood. So if Kripke is right about the essentiality of original constitution then I am *necessarily* flesh and blood: I *could* not have been originally made of gears and wires. But I cannot rule out *a priori* that I *am* a robot: so it might have *turned out* that I am a robot. However if Kripke's interpretation is correct then when I say 'I might have turned out to be a robot', I must be saying that there is a possible world where *a* creature with my evidence *is* a robot. But surely that is wrong. My sceptical worry isn't that there might have been *a* robot with just my evidence (after all, there actually *are* such robots, and that doesn't worry me). What concerns me is that *I* (this very person) might have my actual evidence and yet be a robot. In short: I can use 'It might have turned out that I am a robot' to express a possibility about *me*, not about *a creature* with my evidence. So it cannot be true that the counterpart analysis (a) applies *because* we are interested only in expressing the insecurity of our evidence that the table isn't made from ice. For the statement 'It might have turned out that I am a robot' is also an expression of the insecurity of my evidence. And yet we have as good reason for not applying a counterpart analysis there as we have for withholding it from 'This table might have been transported to the Kremlin'.[9]

The second sentence says that the reason (a) is true but (b) is false is that we already know that the table could *not* have been made of ice. But that too is only an intuition (see 3.1.4): so the position seems to be that we ought to reconstrue the *prima facie* intuition (i) that the table might have been made of ice because we have *another* intuition (ii) that the table could *not* have been made of ice. But that merely shows that we have incompatible intuitions: it is arbitrary to say that we ought to reconstrue (i) in order to save (ii). The situation seems to be this: sometimes we have the intuition (i) and sometimes we have the intuition (ii): and they are genuinely in conflict. The reason that they both seem attractive at times is simply that our modal intuitions are especially malleable (for an example see 3.1.2). But this doesn't mean we have to reconstrue (i) so as to make it consist with (ii). In short: the existence of an intuition that is in conflict with 'This table might have turned out to be made from ice' doesn't by itself mandate an invidious attitude towards them. So our reason for doubting Kripke's account of modal illusion seems to survive both sentences.

To conclude: we saw a reason for doubting Kripke's account of modal illusion. His account of the intuitions behind what he calls modal illusions threatens to make *all* intuitions of contingency equally ill-founded.

3.4 ANTI-MATERIALISM

Psychological events and states include beliefs, desires, hopes and fears; also *phenomenal* events and states like headaches, pins and needles, visual sensations and pains. *Materialism* says that all psychological events and states are physical; *Idealism* that all physical events and states are psychological; and *Dualism* that Idealism and Materialism are both false. Kripke concludes Lecture III by presenting arguments that seem to tell heavily against Materialism (and if they do then similar arguments will be effective against Idealism). This is perhaps the most exciting and certainly the most controversial material in the book.

3.4.1 Kripke's Targets
There are two binary classifications of materialism resulting in four possible positions. These classifications are as follows: (i) type-identity versus token-identity; (ii) theories that apply only to *propositional attitudes* (beliefs, desires, etc.) versus those that apply also to *sensational states* (pain, visual sensations, etc.).

(i) *Token/Type Identification*. Firstly there is the *token-identity* theory. This says that every *particular* psychological state or event is some *particular* physical state or event. The headache that you felt five minutes ago *was* the firing of such-and-such neurons in your brain. The visual hallucinations that you had five minutes before that *were* electrical events in your visual cortex.

Secondly there is the *type-identity* theory. This postulates analyses of psychological states or events in physical terms along the lines of theoretical identifications, e.g. that light is a stream of photons. Each type of psychological state or event is a type of physical state or event: for example, pain may be identified with the stimulation of C-fibres.

If the type-identity theory is true then so is the token-identity theory. If pain *is* the firing of C-fibres then the headache you had five minutes ago *was* some particular C-fibre excitation. But the converse doesn't hold: it may be that token-identity is true but type-identity is false. You could then say that every particular psychological state is *a* physical state while denying that any single type of physical state is common to any two occurrences of the same type of psychological state. An analogy: one might say that every particular smile on a painting *is* a particular configuration of paints on canvas; but there is no *single* type of configuration common to all painted smiles. Davidson held this position for thoughts (1970).

Kripke takes his argument to apply to both token- and type-identity theories (NN2:144n73).

(ii) *Propositional Attitudes/Sensational States.* What Russell calls propositional attitudes – hope, desire, fear, belief and so on – can be distinguished from sensational states on the grounds that the former have no distinctive 'feel': there is nothing 'it is like' to be in one of them. For example: you have presumably believed all your life that the Earth is more than 28 days old. But no particular feeling characterized that state. On the other hand headaches, tickles and itches all *feel* a particular way. There *is* something it is like to suffer them.

Now you might (a) be a materialist (of either the type- or only the token- version) about propositional attitudes while being agnostic about sensational states. Alternatively you might (b) be a materialist about *all* psychological states: you might think that *sensational* as well as propositional attitudinal states and events are physical states or events.[10] Kripke's argument is an objection to position (b). But it has no obvious force against position (a). So when I speak of materialism I shall mean materialism of type (b): the version that entails that sensational states are either individually or also typically identical to physical ones.

Note finally that Kripke's argument differs in the following important respect from Descartes' notorious argument. Descartes concluded that a *person* cannot be identical with any physical object (e.g. his brain or his body). Kripke's argument can show only that psychological *states* and *events* are distinct from physical ones: it says nothing about whether *I* am a material or an immaterial thing (NN:355n77/NN2:155n77).

In short, he takes his argument to undermine *both* of the following: token-materialism of type (b) and type-materialism of type (b). We shall consider its bearing on these positions separately.

3.4.2 The Argument against Token-Materialism

The argument runs as follows. Let 'A' rigidly designate a certain sensational state or event in Jones e.g. a particular pain. And let 'B' rigidly designate an arbitrary physical state or event, e.g. Jones' brain state. Then:

(1) If 'A = B' is true then it is necessarily true (Premise)
(2) It is possible for B to exist without A (Premise)
(3) 'A = B' is not necessarily true (from 2)
(4) A and B are distinct (from 1, 3)

Since B was arbitrary the argument shows that *no* physical state or event – in Jones' brain, his body or the Andromeda Galaxy – is identical to A. Hence A isn't a physical state or event.

As presented, the argument is plainly valid so the only remaining question is whether its premises are true.

3.4.3 Its First Premise

The first premise says that 'A = B' is, if true, necessarily so. We have already seen why Kripke thinks that this statement is necessarily true if true at all (3.1.5). Briefly: if 'A' and 'B' are rigid designators then they each denote the *same* thing at any possible world where they denote at all. Hence if (i) they denote the same thing as one another at @ then (ii) they denote the same thing as one another at all possible worlds. But the truth of 'A = B' entails (i) and the truth of (ii) entails the *necessary* truth of 'A = B'. Hence if 'A = B' is true then it is necessarily true.

It is important to be clear that the argument requires the assumption that 'A' and 'B' both be rigid: it fails if either term is not.[11] Consider the terms 'Benjamin Franklin' and 'The inventor of bifocal lenses'. Whereas the first of these terms is arguably rigid the second most definitely is not: the person who is in fact the inventor of bifocals might have both existed and failed to be the inventor of bifocals. And the statement 'The inventor of bifocals = Benjamin Franklin' is accordingly true but only contingently so. So the analogue of premise (1) fails in this case, as does the argument for it.

One might therefore object to premise (1) on the grounds that it presumes that 'A' and 'B' are rigid designators. Certainly there are non-rigid English expressions that designate what 'A' and 'B' designate (e.g. 'Jones' favourite mental event'). But nothing in the argument for *this* premise turns on that. For nothing in the argument for (1) requires that 'A' and 'B' be expressions of English. As far as the argument is concerned we may as well have *invented* names for the pain and the brain-state ('Alfred' and 'Brian') whose rigidity we *stipulate* (cf. NN:337/NN2:149). The supposition that we do is both weak enough to evade any doubts about the rigidity of 'this pain' and strong enough to entail premise (1).

3.4.4 Its Second Premise: Reasons for Believing It
The second premise says that it is possible that B (which happens to be the brain-state) exists in the absence of A (which happens to be the pain).

Kripke's position seems to be that we have an intuition that it is true: the burden is therefore on the materialist to say why this intuition is misleading. He considers two materialist responses along these lines and argues that neither of them works.

In the following passage Kripke (i) states the *prima facie* case for premise (2); (ii) reaffirms the truth of premise (1); and (iii) considers and rejects *one* reason for doubting premise (2):

> [i] *Prima facie*, it would seem that it is at least logically possible that *B* should have existed (Jones' brain could have been in exactly that state at the time in question) without Jones feeling any pain at all, and thus without the presence of *A*. [ii] Once again, the identity theorist cannot admit the possibility cheerfully and proceed from there; consistency, and the principle of the necessity of identities using rigid designators, disallows any such course. If *A* and *B* were identical, the identity would have to be necessary. [iii] The difficulty can hardly be evaded by arguing

that although *B* could exist without *A*, *being a pain* is merely a contingent property of *A*, and that therefore the presence of *B* without pain does not imply the presence of *B* without *A* … [T]his notion seems to me self-evidently absurd. It amounts to the view that the *very pain I now have* could have existed without being a mental state at all. (NN:335–6/NN2:146–7)

The argument for premise (2) appears under (i). It seems to be this:

(5) It is possible for *B* to exist without pain (Premise)
(2) It is possible for *B* to exist without *A* (from 5)

The premise (5) is motivated by a conversion of the Cartesian thought-experiment: we can imagine Jones not being in pain and yet being in the very brain-state *B* that is supposedly identical to the pain (NN:334/NN2:144–5).

It is puzzling that Kripke here speaks of the *logical* possibility of *B* without pain. We say that *p* is logically possible if it doesn't yield a contradiction by the laws of (first-order predicate) logic alone. But then the mere logical possibility of *B* without pain is too weak to be of interest. The *logical* possibility of *B* without pain can only ever establish the *logical* possibility of *B* without *A*. And logical possibility doesn't entail metaphysical possibility: it is logically but not metaphysically possible that there are married bachelors. So the logical possibility of *B* without *A* is in no conflict with the truth of '*A* = *B*'; for the latter only entails the metaphysical and not the logical necessity of '*A* = *B*'. I therefore propose that we ignore talk of 'logical' possibility in this passage and instead take Kripke to mean metaphysical possibility throughout.

This quibble aside, the plausibility of (5) appears about as great as that of any claim of possibility. Whatever it amounts to, and however we explain it, it seems true both that we *can* conceive of Jones' being in brain-state *B* and yet not being in pain, *and* that we can do so in a way that we normally take to underwrite claims of metaphysical possibility. Let us then accept for the *moment* that premise (5) is true. This then is Kripke's grounds for premise (2) of the main argument.

3.4.5 First Reason for Doubting It

The argument for premise (2) is that it follows from (5). There are two possible responses. The first (Feldman 1974) is to doubt the *validity* of the argument from (5) to (2). The second (McGinn 1977) is to question the truth of (5). In this section I consider the first strategy and at 3.4.6 I consider the second.

The first line of argument is the one that Kripke considers and rejects in the material under (iii) in the passage quoted at 3.4.4.

The materialist who is Kripke's target in (iii) looks at things like this. There is a state of Jones' brain called '*B*' (and also denoted by '*A*'). That state *happens* to be a pain. And indeed just as (5) says, the very same state *could* have existed without being a pain. (Compare: there is a dab of paint on a canvas. It *happens* to be a painted smile, given other facts about what has been painted on the canvas and perhaps the painter's intentions. But of course that very dab might have both existed and failed to be a painted smile, for example if the painter had been distracted before completing the painting or if he had turned the canvas upside down and made it into a painted frown.) But this doesn't mean that at some possible world *B* exists *without A*: for '*A*' (or 'Alfred') names the very same brain-state as '*B*' (or 'Brian') names; and so at any possible world where *B* exists so does *A*. Only at some such worlds neither *B* nor therefore *A* has the contingent property of being a pain.

Against this Kripke maintains that if '*A*' (and also therefore '*B*') names a pain then it names something that *could* not have existed without being one. He gives no argument for this thesis but says only that to deny it is self-evidently absurd.

But the absurdity is hardly self-evident. I myself have *no* intuition that the pain I had yesterday could not have existed without being a pain. In a sense it *is* self-evidently true to say that *that very sensation* could not but have been a pain: but only in the sense that the thing that was a sensation of pain would not have been *that sensation* if it had not been a pain. It doesn't follow, nor is it evident, that it would not have *existed*.

It may be that the following passage (elided in the above quotation) is an invitation to introspection: 'Consider a particular pain, or other sensation, that you once had. Do you find it at all plausible that *that very sensation* could have existed without being a sensation?' So it may be that Kripke is inviting us to verify the claim by looking at our own sensational states.

Well, try it and see. For my own part, focusing on my pain tells me only that it *is* a pain. However minutely I inspect it I see *nothing* to show that it *must* have been a pain, or a sensation. And this introspective blankness is so far as I can tell quite uninformed by any materialistic convictions. It is therefore unclear how anything in the *awareness* of a pain is supposed to tell its owner that it could not but have been one.

It *might* be that this supposedly self-evident assumption is based on two other Berkeleian assumptions: (a) that there is *nothing* to a pain or sensational state other than what we perceive in it when we suffer it; (b) that when one has a pain one perceives in it nothing *but* pain.[12] One might argue from these assumptions that *A* is nothing *but* a pain and therefore any possible item that might reasonably be called 'A' must itself *be* a pain. So (a) and (b) together validate the step from (5) to (2). But the naïvety of both (a) and (b) is quite plain, as are the chances that the token-materialist might grant (a) as a neutral starting point.

So the first reason for doubting premise (2) is a good one. There is no plausible route from (5) to (2).

3.4.6 Second Reason for Doubting It

We saw at 3.4.4 that Kripke has the following argument for premise (2): It is possible for *B* to exist without *A* because (5) it is possible that *B* exists without pain. Another strategy for the materialist would be to reject the premise (5) itself: he might deny that the brain-state dubbed '*B*' *could* exist without pain.

But isn't that implausible? I said at 3.4.4 that we *seem* to have a good reason for believing (5): we can conceive that Jones' brain is in exactly the same state as it actually is though Jones is not in pain. But recall (3.3) that Kripke himself thinks we are sometimes subject to *illusions* of contingency: it seems as though this wooden table might have been made of ice; but all we are really conceiving of is *a* table that looked like this one but was made from ice.

Now the *token*-materialist can proceed in this way. *He* can cheerfully admit that it is conceivable and therefore possible that Jones should have been in *a* brain-state that 'looked' just like his actual brain-state *B* (I assume that we have invented the brain-o-scope and so can determine what *B* looks like). But he denies that we have thereby conceived that *this very* brain-state (which is necessarily a state of pain) should have both existed and failed to be a state of pain. So the token-materialist might consistently hold the following: any *actual* pain A is necessarily identical to some brain-state B; the brain-state B could not possibly have existed without being a pain; but he might also be motivated by the thought-experiment to hold that there could have been *a* brain-state just like B that was *not* a pain. He might even be motivated by the converse and more nearly Cartesian thought-experiment to hold that there could have been *a* pain just like A that wasn't a brain-state. In short, he could grant all of the following:

(a) Any actual pain is such that: necessarily, it is a brain-state
(b) It is possible that: there are brain-states just like B that are not pains
(c) It is possible that: there are pains just like A that are not brain-states

And he would insist that the intuition behind premise (5), and the converse intuition that Jones might have been in pain though his brain-state wasn't what it actually was, do not establish either that B itself might not have been a pain or that A itself might not have been a brain-state. It only establishes that there might have been *a* brain-state just like B that wasn't a pain, and that there might have been *a* pain just like A that wasn't a brain-state. And these claims – (b) and (c) – are altogether compatible with (a).

It is evident from NN:338–40/NN2:151–3 that Kripke thinks that this strategy will *not* help the *type*-identity theorist. And NN:336–7/NN2:148 makes it look as though he thinks similar arguments will apply against the token-identity theory. But as we shall see, his arguments show at best only that the *type*-identity theorist cannot explain away the apparent contingency of the *theoretical identification* of a certain type of psychological state (pain) with a certain type of physical state (the firing of C-fibres). To anticipate somewhat, his argument is this:

> To be in the same epistemic situation that would obtain if one has a pain *is* to have a pain; to be in the same epistemic situation that would obtain in the absence of pain *is* not to have a pain. The apparent contingency of the connection between the [mental] state and the corresponding brain state thus cannot be

explained by some sort of qualitative analogue as in the case of heat. (NN:339/NN2:152)

But of course the token-identity theorist can perfectly well grant that Jones might have been in a state of pain *qualitatively* identical with *A* without being in the brain-state *B*; all he denies is that we are thereby imagining Jones to be in a state of pain that is *numerically* identical with *A*.

It seems therefore that the token-identity theory can never be threatened by Kripke's arguments. A token-identity theorist might hold *either* that the appearance that *this* brain-state might not have been *that* pain is an illusion; or he might hold that even if it is *not* an illusion it entails neither the possible nor the actual distinctness of the brain-state *B* and the pain *A*. In either case he can reject premise (2) of Kripke's overall argument.

3.4.7 The Argument against Type-Materialism

The type-materialist holds not only that every particular psychological state or event is a physical state or event but also that any two events of the same *psychological* type are events of the same *physical* type. Thus it is compatible with token-materialism but not type-materialism that two occurrences of the same type of pain are occurrences of distinct types of neural state. There is therefore a precise parallel between type-materialism and such theoretical identifications as that between light and streams of photons or that between water and hydrogen hydroxide (NN:337/NN2:148). The typical identification that Kripke discusses is that between pain and the stimulation of C-fibres.

The argument against type-materialism is stated as follows:

It should be clear from the previous discussion that 'pain' is a rigid designator of the type, or phenomenon, it designates: if something is a pain it is essentially so, and it seems absurd to suppose that pain could have been some phenomenon other than the one it is. The same holds for the term 'C-fibre stimulation', provided that 'C-fibres' is a rigid designator, as I will suppose here ... Thus the identity of pain with the stimulation of C-fibres, if true, must be *necessary*. (NN:337/NN2:148–9)

This argument may be stated as follows:

(6) If 'Pain is C-fibre stimulation' is necessarily true then there could not have been C-fibre stimulations without pains (Premise)

(7) If 'Pain is C-fibre stimulation' is true then it is necessarily true (Premise)

(8) There could have been C-fibre stimulations without pains (Premise)

(9) 'Pain is C-fibre stimulation' is not necessarily true (from 6, 8)

(10) Pain and C-fibre stimulation are distinct (from 7, 9)

As written, the argument is valid. And it is difficult to deny its first premise. Recall that the disputed claim 'Pain is C-fibre stimulation' is meant to be understood along the lines of 'Water is H_2O' and therefore not as an *identity*-statement but as a *theoretical identification* (3.2.4). The antecedent of (6) therefore says that necessarily, anything that is an instance of C-fibre firing is also an instance of pain. So any possible C-fibre firing is an instance of pain; hence there could not have been an instance of C-fibre firing that wasn't an instance of pain.

It follows that there are two and only two ways for the type-materialist to respond. He might reject the second premise (Lewis 1980a); or he might reject the third premise (Boyd 1980).

3.4.8 Its Second Premise

Kripke's ground for the second premise appears to be that since both 'pain' and 'C-fibre stimulation' are rigid designators their identification must be necessary.

But what grounds are there for thinking that 'pain' *rigidly* designates a certain type of phenomenon? Kripke's own position is that the contrary is intuitively absurd: it seems 'absurd to suppose that pain could have been some phenomenon other than the one it is'.

But this is *not* absurd. Why could it not have happened that the phenomenon that is in fact pain might have been the very same phenomenon without yet being pain? And if that *could* have been the case then it could have been true that the phenomenon of C-fibre stimulation might only *contingently* be (and yet for all that still *be*) pain. That is the position of a functionalist like Lewis, for whom pain is that physical state that is both caused by blows to the head and itself causes aversion and distress. He thinks that that (type of) physical state both is and might not have been pain:

> If the state of having neurons hooked up in a certain way and firing in a certain pattern is the state properly apt for causing and being caused, as we materialists think, then that neural state is pain. But the concept of pain is not the concept of that neural state. The concept of pain, unlike the concept of the neural state which is in fact pain, would have applied to some different state if the relevant causal relations had been different. Pain might not have been pain. (Lewis 1980a:218)

To speak for myself I feel no intuitive pull contrary to this: so I see no reason to doubt that what is in fact pain might not have been, and hence that 'pain' does not denote rigidly.

It may be argued (Hughes 2004:212) that the non-rigidity of pain is irrelevant: instead of 'pain' we may use 'that kind of feeling'. Since 'that kind of feeling' designates rigidly by virtue of the demonstrative 'that', it will designate the very same feeling – pain – at all possible worlds. Hence if 'that kind of feeling is C-fibre stimulation' is true it is necessary. But *does* the presence of the demonstrative ensure rigidity in this case? 'That kind of feeling' rigidly designates a certain phenomenon only if the following is false: 'the phenomenon that is in fact that kind of feeling might have both existed and failed to be that kind of feeling'. But the materialist will think, reasonably enough, that this is *true*. On his view the only phenomena around to be designated are physical ones: 'that kind of feeling' may designate some such phenomenon, but in other possible worlds where that physical phenomenon exists it may not.

Now there is *a* sense in which 'pain' can perhaps be said to be rigid (see 3.2.4). A rigid designator of a kind is in this sense not one that *refers* in all possible worlds to the phenomenon or property that it actually refers to but rather one that *applies* in all possible worlds to any particular thing that it actually applies to. Thus 'heat' is rigid if any instance of heat could not have both existed and failed to be heat. And 'pain' is rigid if anything that is in fact an instance of pain could not have both existed and failed to be a pain. We saw at 3.4.5 reasons to doubt that 'pain' *is* rigid in this attenuated sense.

But even if 'C-fibre stimulation' and 'pain' are both rigid in this sense, all that follows is this:

(11) If 'pain is C-fibre stimulation' is true, then nothing that is *actually* either could have both existed and failed to be both

But (11) is weaker than (7): for the type-materialist who grants (11), unlike the one who grants (7), can maintain that there might have been *a* C-fibre stimulation that wasn't a pain, so long as he grants that no *actual* stimulation might have both existed and failed to be a pain. And this is fatal to the overall argument: for whereas (10) does follow from (7) and (9), it doesn't follow from (11) and (9). (This vindicates my claim at the end of 3.2.4 that this notion of rigidity is of no use to Kripke in his argument against theoretical identifications of mental and physical phenomena.)

So it remains unclear why the type-identity theorist should grant the second premise of Kripke's argument against him.

3.4.9 Its Third Premise
Can the type-identity theorist reject the premise that there might have been C-fibre stimulations that are not pains? If so he must account for the apparent conceivability of Jones' suffering C-fibre stimulations without being in pain.

Note that the strategy offered to the token-identity theorist at 3.4.6 isn't available here: not, at any rate, if Kripke's premises (6) and (7) are true. It isn't open to the *type*-identity theorist to admit that we can imagine *a* brain-state that is like Jones' actual brain-state and yet isn't a pain, but to insist that any *actual* such brain-state is necessarily a pain. *He* is committed not just to the thesis that any *actual* brain-state of that type is necessarily a pain, but also (by premises (6) and (7)) to the stronger thesis that there could not be *a* brain-state of that type that isn't a pain. But this is just what we seem able to imagine.

Now we saw at 3.3.1 that Kripke sought to explain away the apparent contingency of 'Heat is molecular motion' along the following lines. When we think we are imagining an instance of molecular motion that isn't an instance of heat, what we are *really* imagining is an instance of molecular motion that doesn't *feel* like heat. But to imagine molecular motion without the feeling of heat isn't yet to imagine molecular motion in the *absence* of heat: so it doesn't follow from the thought-experiment that the identification of heat and molecular motion is contingent.

We also saw that this approach could be generalized in the following way. Given a theoretical identification 'X is Y', and definite descriptions D1 and D2 to pick out X and Y respectively, one's apparent conceiving of the distinctness of X and Y could be explained away as the genuine conceiving, not of *that*, but rather as one of the following three things:

(a) A possible world where the thing that satisfies D1 is distinct from Y
(b) A possible world where the thing that satisfies D2 is distinct from X
(c) A possible world where the thing that satisfies D1 is distinct from the thing that satisfies D2

Now (granting the contestable rigidity of 'pain') can we use this approach to explain away the apparent conceivability of C-fibre stimulation without pain? To do so would be to reconstrue that apparent conceiving as a genuine conceiving not of pain, but as one of the following:

(d) A possible world where the thing that is picked out in the way that we actually pick out pain is distinct from C-fibre stimulation
(e) A possible world where the thing that is picked out in the way that we actually pick out C-fibre stimulation is distinct from pain
(f) A possible world where the thing that is picked out in the way that we actually pick out pain is distinct from the thing that is picked out in the way that we actually pick out C-fibre stimulation

So, can we reconstrue the apparent conceiving of C-fibre stimulation without pain as a genuine conceiving of one of (d)–(f)?

Kripke argues not, as follows:

Pain ... is not picked out by one of its accidental properties; rather it is picked out by the property of being pain itself, by its immediate phenomenological quality. Thus pain, unlike heat, is not only rigidly designated by 'pain' but the reference of the designator is determined by an essential property of the referent. Thus it is not possible to say that although pain is necessarily identical with a certain physical state, a certain phenomenon can be picked out in the same way we pick out pain without being correlated with that physical state. If any phenomenon is picked out in exactly the same way that we pick out pain, then that phenomenon *is* pain. (NN:339–40/NN2:152–3)

In short: to conceive of something picked out in the way that we actually pick out pain (or its absence: NN:339/NN2:152) *is* to conceive of pain (or its absence). Hence construal (d) gets us no further: the possible world described in (d) just *is* a possible world where pain is distinct from C-fibre stimulations.

There are three objections to this.

Objection (i) (Boyd 1980:84–5). Even if Kripke's argument rules out (d) as a (type-) materialistically acceptable reconstrual of the thought experiment, it doesn't rule out (e) or (f). Could we not grant that we really are imagining that Jones isn't in *pain*, but insist that it is not *C-fibre* stimulation that we are imagining to be going on in Jones but only something that *resembles* it? It is after all plausible that C-fibre stimulation (though not pain) is picked out by one of *its* contingent features, e.g. how it appears on a brain-o-scope. All we are imagining is that Jones isn't in pain while at the same time the brain-o-scope says that his C-fibres *are* firing. It is then compatible with the content of our imagining that his C-fibres are in fact *not* firing.

The difficulty with this is that it is on a line of thought whose terminus is that we can never conceive of *anything* other than how things might appear to us (Wright 2002:413–7). Surely there is a difference between conceiving e.g. that I am suffering from the illusion that I do not have a hand and conceiving that in fact I do *not* have a hand. But if so then there is also a difference between conceiving that it misleadingly *seems* as though Jones' C-fibres are firing and conceiving that they are *actually* firing. (If not then it is difficult to avoid the conclusion that we ever conceive of anything other than how things appear to us.) But then it seems perfectly possible to conceive of the latter without conceiving of the former: it seems that we can imagine that Jones' C-fibres *are* really firing. And if we can conceive of that then we can also conceive at the same time that Jones is feeling no pain. *This* thought experiment cannot be reconstrued in terms of (e) or (f), at least not if (e) or (f) describe possible worlds where the brain-o-scope is misleading. The only alternative is to construe it as (d): a world where whatever is picked out in the way that pain actually is is absent even though C-fibre stimulation is really present. And that is of no help: as Kripke argued, we *cannot* conceive that our ordinary criterion for pain (or its absence) should be both satisfied and misleading.

Objection (ii). But is that last point really correct? Is it not possible that we can imagine Jones being by our ordinary criteria in no pain even though he *is* in pain?

We have to distinguish the following two things: imagining that *Jones* is in no pain, and imagining that *I* feel no pain *in Jones' body* (as one might feel no pain in one's leg: cf. W:129). It is the former and not the latter that we are supposed to be imagining. And while it is true that I pick out *my* pain via a criterion that cannot mislead, the same is *not* true of Jones' pain. *We* don't fix the reference of 'Jones' pain' by means of 'its immediate phenomenological quality': Jones' pain has for us *no* such quality. We rather fix its reference by means of Jones' behaviour: it is what makes him cry out, etc. And of course this *is* a contingent feature of Jones' pain: he might have been showing no signs of pain and yet still have been in pain.

It is therefore open to the materialist to say this. When you think you are conceiving that Jones isn't in pain but his C-fibres are being stimulated, you are actually conceiving not *that* but rather one of the following two things:

(g) At some possible world Jones' C-fibres are being stimulated but *you* feel no pain in his body

(h) At some possible world Jones' C-fibres are being stimulated but he does not satisfy the criteria by which we actually fix the reference of Jones' pain, i.e. he does not exhibit characteristic pain-behaviour

And it doesn't follow from either of these that we can imagine that Jones isn't in pain when his C-fibres are being stimulated. It doesn't follow from (g) because Jones might feel pain in his body even though you do not. And it doesn't follow from (h) because Jones might feel pain even though he doesn't show it.

The obvious response is to dispense with Jones altogether. *I* can imagine that *I* feel no pain even though *my* C-fibres are being stimulated. And the one and only criterion by which I fix the reference of 'my (present) pain' *is* its immediate phenomenological quality;[13] so there can be no gap between imagining that the criterion is not satisfied and imagining that I am not in pain. It is therefore upon a thought experiment about oneself (and not Jones) that the third premise of Kripke's argument must rely. It remains to be seen whether he *can* rely on it: and this brings us to the third objection.

Objection (iii). The third objection is in two parts. Firstly: is it really possible to conceive of a world where *I* am feeling no pain and in which *my* C-fibres are being stimulated? The materialist need not admit this, for he can reconstrue the supposed conceiving. He can say that what we are really conceiving is not *that* but only a world where I feel no pain but where the C-fibres that are being stimulated are not *mine*. We can certainly imagine a world where C-fibre stimulation is going on *somewhere*: but something more needs to be true there for it to be one where *my* C-fibres are being stimulated. It isn't sufficient that those C-fibres be contained within *my* body: there are possible worlds where someone *else's* C-fibres (the ones that cause him pain) happen to be contained in my body (the one that I control) – cf. Siamese twins. The materialist is within his rights to insist that the only C-fibres in any world that can reasonably be called 'mine' are those whose stimulation is there correlated with *my* feeling pain. But then he can maintain that I cannot imagine a world where *I* feel no pain despite stimulation of *my* C-fibres.

However the materialist has no such defence against the converse and more nearly Cartesian thought experiment. It is surely possible to imagine that I *am* feeling pain and yet where *no* C-fibres (and hence not *my* C-fibres, *whichever* ones those are) are being stimulated. The conceivability of *that* world appears both obvious and damaging to type-materialism. This brings me to the second part of the objection.

It is surely impossible that there be auditory experiences in a world containing no sentient beings. And yet this seems to be conceivable. We can conceive e.g. of the sound made by a falling tree in a world containing only vegetables: this might be portrayed in a film. Does it follow that there might have been auditory experiences in a world containing only vegetables?

Surely not. The appearance can be defused by reconstruing the apparent conceiving of auditory experiences in a world containing only vegetables as a *genuine* conceiving of something *else*. What we are conceiving is not that but rather *what* a falling tree in a vegetable-world *would* sound like to a sentient being (with ears). It doesn't follow that we cannot conceive of a vegetable-world any more than that such a world cannot be depicted in a movie. It is rather that we conceive of a vegetable-world *by* imagining what it would sound (and look) like.

Now this kind of reconstrual is available to the materialist. He can insist that what we thought was a conceiving of pain-experience in a world without C-fibres is not quite *that*. It is rather a conceiving of *what* such a world would feel like to a suitably placed creature that *was* equipped with C-fibres. I can imagine, for example, a world without C-fibres (and even without brains) where I am pricked with a pin. And I can imagine at the same time *what* that would feel (and look) like if I *did* have a brain and C-fibres. But we are not thereby imagining *that* I am both brainless and yet in pain any more than we are imagining auditory experiences in the vegetable-world. The thought-experiment doesn't therefore show that I might have been in pain in the absence of C-fibres.

The challenge to the anti-materialist is therefore to say what feature of the Cartesian thought-experiment prohibits this reconstrual of it. I am hardly confident that no such feature can be found. But unless the Cartesian thought-experiment is described in more detail its content at least *appears* re-describable in a way that the type-materialist should find acceptable.

3.4.10 Conclusion

I distinguished four positions: token-materialism of type (a), type-materialism of type (a), token-materialism of type (b) and type-materialism of type (b). Neither materialism of type (a) is even *prima facie* vulnerable to Kripke's arguments. What about token- and type-materialism of type (b)?

We saw at 3.4.2 that Kripke has a valid argument against token-materialism of type (b). The argument had two premises, there labelled (1) and (2). We saw at 3.4.3 that the first premise – that '$A = B$' is necessarily true if true at all – was plausible. But premise (2) – that B could exist without A – was questionable. We saw at 3.4.4 that Kripke sought to derive it from the assumption there labelled (5) – that *B* could exist without pain. But I argued at 3.4.5 that (2) does *not* follow from (5), and at 3.4.6 that the token-materialist can in any case question (5) itself by reconstruing the thought-experiment behind it.

We saw at 3.4.7 that Kripke has a valid argument against *type*-materialism whose first premise – that if it is necessary that pain is the stimulation of C-fibres then there could not have been a C-fibre stimulation that wasn't a pain – was plausible. But both the other premises were questionable. Premise (7) – that if 'pain is C-fibre stimulation' is true then it is necessary – rested on the assumption that 'pain' is rigid. But I argued at 3.4.8 that 'pain' is plausibly rigid only in a sense of 'rigidity' that doesn't support (7) but only the weaker premise that if pain is C-fibre stimulation then no *actual* C-fibre stimulation could have both existed and yet not been a pain. And this premise is useless against the materialist. Premise (8) – that there might have been C-fibre stimulation without pain, or vice versa – was questioned at 3.4.9. The first objection was that the intuition behind it could be regarded as a modal illusion by adopting Kripke's strategy of reconstrual as outlined at 3.3.1. This was found unpersuasive. The second objection was that we *can* reconstrue the intuition that somebody *else* might have felt pain (no pain) in the absence (presence) of C-fibre stimulation in a way that is acceptable to the materialist. And the third objection was that we can also reconstrue the intuition that *I* might have felt pain in the absence of C-fibre stimulation in a way that is acceptable to the materialist. Taken together, these last two objections provide *prima facie* but hardly conclusive grounds for rejecting Kripke's third premise; in any case I believe that 3.4.8 gave firm reasons for rejecting the second.

It seems therefore that *none* of the four forms of materialism distinguished at 3.4.1 is vulnerable to Kripke's arguments. They could never apply to materialism of type (a). And both type- and token-materialist of type (b) could reasonably regard them as unsound.

3.5 SUMMARY

In this chapter we saw Kripke arguing for the following:

(1) It makes sense to speak of essential properties of individuals however described
(2) Given (1), individual persons essentially have their actual ancestors
(3) Given (1), material objects essentially have their actual material origin
(4) Given (1), material objects essentially have their original material constitution
(5) Given (1), identical/distinct individuals are necessarily so
(6) Statements of identity/distinctness involving rigid designators are necessarily true if true at all
(7) Its associated phenomenal properties are neither *a priori* necessary nor sufficient for membership of a natural kind
(8) Natural kinds have certain properties essentially
(9) From (7) and maybe (8) it follows that antidescriptivism with regard to proper names applies also to natural kind terms
(10) Theoretical identifications are if true at all necessarily so
(11) If X and Y are the same then the only sense in which 'it could have turned out X and Y are distinct' can be true is this: that the descriptions by which we actually pick them out might have failed to coincide
(12) Failure to grasp (11) is a source of modal illusion
(13) The falsity of token-materialism follows from (6) and (11)
(14) The falsity of type-materialism follows from (10) and (11)

It seems that Kripke has given solid grounds for (5), (6) and (7). But we saw that his arguments for all the other claims may be questioned.

4

RULE-FOLLOWING

We now turn to *Wittgenstein on Rules and Private Language*. I want to make two initial points about this book.

Firstly, the views in it are not all Kripke's:

> The primary purpose of this work is the presentation of a problem and an argument, not its critical evaluation. Primarily I can be read, except in a few obvious asides, as almost like an attorney presenting a major philosophical argument as it struck me. (W: ix)

Secondly, the book isn't primarily intended as exegesis of *Wittgenstein* either. Kripke is instead 'trying to present ... that set of arguments which I have personally gotten out of reading Wittgenstein', principally *Philosophical Investigations* (W:5). The relation between Kripke and Wittgenstein's text is that between the patient and the Rorschach spot (Baker and Hacker 1984:2): Kripke's writings derive from but do not represent Wittgenstein's. In the following I pay no attention to the question of Kripke's fidelity to Wittgenstein. But some passages in Wittgenstein's work give pithy expression to positions described by Kripke and I quote these where necessary.

Accordingly when I say 'Kripke thinks X' or 'Kripke says Y' I won't normally mean either that Kripke thinks X or that Kripke says that *Wittgenstein* thinks Y. Without any indication to the contrary the reader should instead understand these phrases only as introducing the views explicitly presented in Kripke's text. The exception to this rule will be 5.1.3. There it will be necessary to distinguish both Kripke's and Wittgenstein's views from those that the text attributes to Wittgenstein.

4.1 THE SCEPTICAL CHALLENGE

The entirety of W revolves around a single problem that is easy to state but hard to answer. Here I state the problem and then outline the constraints placed on an acceptable answer.

4.1.1 Its Nature

Every Anglophone knows that 'plus' means addition. So 'seven plus five' denotes what you get if you add seven and five, i.e. 12. And everyone knows how to add. So every Anglophone knows what answer to give (or how to go about finding it) if asked a question of the form 'x plus y' where x and y are replaced by arabic numerals. The answer is the *sum* of x and y and can be written '$x + y$'.

None of us has added more than finitely many pairs of numbers. But every number is smaller than some; so there are pairs of numbers both of which are higher than either of any pair whose sum you *have* computed. We suppose from now on that 68 and 57 form such a pair.

Not every Anglophone knows what 'quus' means. We define 'quus' to denote the mathematical operation of *quaddition* which we write '*'. This in turn is defined as follows:

$$x * y = x + y \text{ if } x, y < 57$$
$$x * y = 5 \text{ otherwise}$$

So if x and y are both less than 57 then $x * y$ is the same as $x + y$. Otherwise they may differ. And when $(x, y) = (68, 57)$ they *will* differ, since $68 + 57 = 125$ whereas $68 * 57 = 5$ (W:9).

We know that you have not yet added numbers greater than 56. So all your previous answers to queries of the form 'x plus y' would have been the same if you had meant *quaddition*, not *addition*. Then the sceptical challenge is this: what fact is there in virtue of which you meant *addition* rather than *quaddition* by 'plus'?

Here is a way to dramatize it. Suppose persons A and B have throughout their lives been asked the same questions of the form 'x plus y' and given the same answers. Suppose that neither of them has ever computed the answer to any such question for any x or y

greater than 56. Suppose finally that A meant addition by 'plus' and B meant *quaddition*. Then the sceptic asks: what difference must there have been between A and B? If no essential difference can be found then there is no fact in virtue of which A meant addition rather than quaddition by 'plus'. If you (or God) list all the facts in the universe there need be nothing in the list to distinguish A from B. It is just this possibility for A that the sceptic is raising as a possibility for you.

I stress that the debate isn't about whether there are arithmetical facts. We all agree at the outset that there is a fact about whether 68 plus 57 is or was 125. That is not in question. What *is* in question is whether there is any fact in virtue of which '68 plus 57' as you *meant* it in the past denoted 125 or 5 (W:12).

It should also be emphasized that the problem isn't epistemological. It isn't: how do you (with your limitations on memory) know what you meant? (See W:39.) Nor is it: how does somebody else (who cannot see into your mind) know what you meant? (W:14.) The problem is metaphysical: what fact is there in virtue of which you meant addition? Kripke sometimes puts it like this: how can *God* know that you meant addition? (See e.g. W:38.) So stated, it is not a problem of superlunary epistemology but one of sublunary metaphysics. If even God, who can see all the facts about the past (and into your mind), could not know that you meant addition then that doesn't illustrate limitations on God's knowledge. It shows that there is in this case *no* fact *for* him to know.

In Chapter 2 of W Kripke goes through a variety of candidate facts that might constitute your having meant addition by 'plus'. And he argues that none of them constitutes it. Hence there is no fact in virtue of which you meant addition by plus (W:55, 70–1).

4.1.2 Its Significance
The significance of the problem is apparent once you see how it generalizes. If it can be shown that there *was* no fact in virtue of which you *meant* addition by 'plus' then it can be shown that there *is* no fact in virtue of which you *mean* addition by it (W:13). The sceptic is at this stage taking for granted that you *now* mean addition by 'plus' only so as not to jeopardize the meaningfulness of the *present* debate (W:11–12).

But if it can be shown that there is no fact in virtue of which *you* mean addition then it can be shown that there is no fact in virtue of which *anyone* means addition by 'plus'. And there is nothing special about 'plus' – if scepticism about 'plus' is irrefutable then so is scepticism about any word in any language. This obviously holds for words that have more potential than actual applications: for any such word a quus-like alternative meaning could easily be devised. Indeed the problem arises even for words that have been applied in all possible contexts (W:52n34). Suppose e.g. that by yesterday we had answered every possible query of the form '*x* plus *y*': we have computed the sum of every one of the infinitely many pairs of numbers. We may define the *schmaddition* function % as follows, letting *t* be today's date:

$$x \% y = x + y \text{ if computed before } t$$
$$x \% y = x * y \text{ otherwise}$$

Then even somebody who has in the past answered *all* possible queries of the form '*x* plus *y*' will face the question of whether in the past he meant addition or schmaddition. If no facts can be cited to answer this question then no facts will make it true, even of this infinite being, that he meant either.

In short, the sceptical challenge has this profound implication: if it cannot be answered then there are *never* any facts about what *anyone* means by *anything*!

4.1.3 The Normativity Constraint

I stated the sceptical challenge as a *single* question: what facts were there as to whether I meant addition rather than quaddition by 'plus'? But Kripke sometimes represents the sceptic as asking *two* questions:

> In the discussion below the challenge posed by the sceptic takes two forms. First, he questions whether there is any fact that I meant plus, not quus, that will answer his sceptical challenge. Second, he questions whether I have any reason to be so confident that now I should answer '125' rather than '5'. (W:11)

In fact the second question just introduces a constraint on any answer to the first. The nature of this constraint appears from the following.

Why are you confident that if now asked about '68 plus 57' you should say '125' rather than '5'? That confidence rests on three alleged facts. (i) You intend *now* to mean by 'plus' what you meant by it in the past. (ii) Your having meant addition by 'plus' in the past is something of which you are now aware. (iii) Your present awareness of what you meant somehow *directs* you to say '125'. Now the sceptic thinks that any fact as to what you meant in the past by 'plus' must satisfy the following constraint: present awareness of it must *tell* you how to respond to '68 plus 57'. Hence by questioning the existence of any such fact in the past the sceptic is questioning whether anything that you are now aware of tells you how to respond to the present query '68 plus 57'. And by questioning *this* the sceptic is putting in jeopardy fact (iii), and hence also your present confidence that '125' is the right answer.

The nature of this constraint is confirmed by what follows in the quoted passage:

> The two forms of the challenge are related. I am confident that I should answer '125' because I am confident that this answer also accords with what I *meant*. Neither the accuracy of my computation nor of my memory is under dispute. So it ought to be agreed that *if* I meant plus, then unless I wish to change my usage, I am justified in answering (indeed compelled to answer) '125', not '5'. An answer to the sceptic must satisfy two conditions. First, it must give an account of what fact it is (about my mental state) that constitutes my meaning plus, not quus. But further, there is a condition that any putative candidate for such a fact must satisfy. It must, in some sense, show how I am justified in giving the answer '125' to '68 + 57' ... Otherwise, the sceptic has not been answered when he holds that my present response is arbitrary. (W:11)

To state the constraint more briefly: any fact in virtue of which you meant addition by 'plus' must tell you how to answer a novel addition problem. This is known in the literature as the *normativity requirement*. So stated, it is open to more than one interpretation. Because of its central place in Kripke's exposition it is important that we get clear on what it really amounts to.

One interpretation is this: Kripke's sceptic demands that any fact you cite must be one in virtue of which *there is* a right and a wrong answer to '68 plus 57'. Here is Boghossian's very clear statement of that idea:

Suppose the expression 'green' means *green*. It follows immediately that the expression 'green' applies correctly only to *these* things (the green ones) and not to those (the non-greens). The fact that the expression means something implies, that is, a whole set of normative truths about my behaviour with that expression: namely, that my use of it is correct in application of it to some objects and not in application to others. (Boghossian 1989:148)[1]

On this reading the normativity requirement would be met by any fact that ensured the difference between a right and a wrong answer to '68 plus 57' *whether or not* that fact justified *me* in answering '125' rather than '5'. Call this the *external normativity requirement* (ENR).

But I think Kripke means something stronger than that. What he means isn't just that any fact that answers the sceptic must make a difference between right and wrong: it must be a fact awareness of which *guides* your responses in one direction rather than another.[2] Call this the *internal normativity requirement* (INR). It is worth saying something about the grounds and consequences of this attribution.

What is my evidence that Kripke accepts INR? I have two grounds for it. Firstly, at 14 points in the book he advertises his sceptic's conclusion using metaphors of vision and guidance. The sceptic's conclusion is that novel applications of 'plus' are a *leap in the dark* (W:10, 17, 55). When you answer '68 plus 57' you are operating *blindly* (W:17, 81n70, 87). Nothing *guides* you to say '125' rather than '5' (W:17, 56, 103n83).[3] These metaphors make perfect sense if the gist of the sceptical argument is that no fact meets the *internal* normativity requirement. But they are quite misplaced if his point is that no fact meets the external normativity requirement. For that requirement says nothing about whether putative meaning-facts might *tell* you the right answer; only that putative meaning-facts ensure that some answer *is* right. Hence the distinctive content of the claim that no fact meets the external normativity requirement is not appropriately expressed in terms of blindness, leaps in the dark, etc. It is possible that although there *is* a fact guaranteeing a right answer to '68 plus 57' (and hence ENR is satisfied), *still* nothing guides you there.

My second piece of evidence is that many of Kripke's arguments are invalid unless we assume INR as a premise. This will become clearer when we consider those arguments in detail.

One consequence of the attribution is that INR plays a central role in arguing against *all* the candidate answers to the sceptic. As Kripke says:

> Exactly how this [normativity] condition operates will become much clearer below, after we discuss Wittgenstein's paradox on an intuitive level, when we consider various philosophical theories as to what the fact that I meant plus might consist in. There will be many specific objections to these theories. But all fail to give a candidate for a fact as to what I meant that would show that only '125', not '5', is the answer I 'ought' to give. (W:11)

Thus we can impose a very clear structure on the argument of Chapter 2. For each fact F that is proposed as the fact in virtue of which I meant addition by 'plus', Kripke's argument will have the following schematic appearance:

(1) If F is the fact in virtue of which you meant addition by 'plus', F will satisfy INR (Premise)
(2) F does not satisfy INR (Premise)
(3) Therefore, F is not the fact in virtue of which you meant addition by 'plus' (from 1, 2)

We shall see repeated instances of this pattern at 4.2 and 4.3: in fact five of the 14 arguments that we consider proceed like this.

The second consequence of attributing INR to Kripke is that it puts him in a relatively traditional context. On my interpretation the basic thought of Chapter 2 of W is that no object of awareness can guide my actions. W can therefore be viewed as continuing a line of thought that runs via Wittgenstein and Schopenhauer[4] back to Berkeley's view that the will is not an idea.[5] It is Wittgenstein who captures it most vividly:

> Make some arbitrary doodle on a bit of paper. – And now make a copy next to it, let yourself be guided by it. – I should like to say: 'Sure enough, I was guided here. But as for what was characteristic in what happened, I no longer find it characteristic.' But now notice this: *while* I am being guided everything is

quite simple, I notice nothing special; but afterwards, when I ask myself what it was that happened, it seems to me to have been something indescribable. *Afterwards* no description satisfies me ... 'For surely,' I tell myself, 'I was being *guided*.' – Only then does the idea of that ethereal, intangible influence arise. When I look back on the experience I have the feeling that what is essential about it is an 'experience of being influenced', of a connexion – as opposed to mere simultaneity of phenomena: but at the same time I should not be willing to call any experienced phenomenon the 'experience of being influenced'. (This contains the germ of the idea that the will is not a *phenomenon*.) I should like to say that I had experienced the '*because*', and yet I do not want to call any phenomenon the 'experience of the because'. (1967: sections 175–6)

Here is Chapter 2 of W in a nutshell.

4.2 POSSIBLE ANSWERS TO IT

In Chapter 2 Kripke considers and rejects six candidate facts in virtue of which you meant addition by 'plus'. These are: assimilation of a rule (15–18); dispositionalism (22–37); simplicity (38–40); introspectible mental states (41–6); *sui generis* facts (51–3); and Platonic abstract objects (53–4). In this section I describe and assess what Kripke says about five of these. Dispositionalism will be held over to the next section.

4.2.1 Assimilation of a Rule
The immediate reply to the sceptic is that of course he is unanswerable if one looks only at one's previous responses to *particular* queries of the form '*x* plus *y*'. By hypothesis these are all compatible with your having meant quaddition rather than addition all along. What makes it true that you meant addition is rather this: you were aware of the *rule* for 'plus'. Kripke states the point and describes an example as follows:

Surely I did not merely give myself some finite number of examples, from which I am supposed to extrapolate the whole table [for 'plus'] ... Rather I learned – and internalized instructions for

– a *rule* which determines how addition is to be continued. What was the rule? Well, say, to take it in its most primitive form: suppose we wish to add *x* and *y*. Take a huge bunch of marbles. First count out *x* marbles in a heap. Then count out *y* marbles in another. Put the two heaps together and count out the number of marbles in the union thus formed. The result is *x* + *y*. This set of directions, I may suppose, I explicitly gave myself at some earlier time. It is engraved on my mind as on a slate. It is incompatible with the hypothesis that I meant quus. It is this set of directions, not the finite list of particular additions, that justifies and determine my present response. (W:15–16)

This passage actually contains *two* suggested responses to the sceptic. The first is that your meaning addition by 'plus' consisted in your having heard or vocalized *words* that state the rule in question. The second – indicated by the claim that the rule is 'internalized' or 'engraved on my mind' – is that your meaning consisted in your possessing some *mental* representation of the rule.

Kripke's response to the first suggestion is swift and decisive. The words used in the explicit instructions do not by themselves guide your response to '68 plus 57' because they (just like the word 'plus' itself) are also open to scepticism:

Thus the sceptic can question my present interpretation of my past usage of 'count' as he did with 'plus'. In particular, he can claim that by 'count' I formerly meant *quount*, where to 'quount' a heap is to count it in the ordinary sense, unless the heap was formed as the union of two heaps, one of which has 57 or more items, in which case one must automatically give the answer '5'. (W:16)

In short: nothing in the verbal statement of a rule can guide you to say '125' rather than '5': for nothing in that statement can tell you that on this occasion you are supposed to *count* rather than to *quount* the marbles. The proposal therefore fails to meet INR.

Kripke doesn't directly address the second suggestion – that your having meant addition by 'plus' consisted not in *verbal* instructions but in your possessing some *mental* state encoding the rule. The fact that an English word like 'count' admits of quus-like interpretation can never tell against this: that the hearing of such a word prompted you to enter a mental state is purely adventitious as far as the content of the latter is concerned. But it is obvious enough what the sceptic would say. The supposed complex mental state or configuration embodying grasp of the rule must involve some component M that means counting rather than quounting. And then Kripke can play the same sceptical game with M as he did with 'count': what is there about it that tells me to count rather than to quount?

We will go over this second argument in more detail when we consider Kripke's extended attack, much later in Chapter 2, on the suggestion that meaning addition by 'plus' is an introspectible mental state (see 4.2.3–5). For the moment we can conclude as follows. Kripke has given decisive reasons for denying that your having meant addition by 'plus' consisted in some past *verbalization* of the rule for 'plus'. And he has given a *prima facie* reason for denying that it consisted in your having had some *mental* representation of it.

4.2.2 Simplicity

It is natural to think that in some sense addition is *simpler* than quaddition. We can define addition but not quaddition by a simple rule. And we often appeal to simplicity to help us decide between competing hypotheses. For example, the heliocentric Copernican model of the Solar System may be preferred on these grounds to the geocentric Ptolemaic one, even if the latter is so refined that it is just as compatible with astronomical observation as the former. Might we not on similar grounds prefer the hypothesis that you meant addition? We could then respond to the sceptic as follows: what makes it true that you meant addition rather than quaddition by 'plus' is that the former is the simpler hypothesis.

Kripke thinks this may be refuted on grounds that are quite independent of the vagueness of 'simpler' (which he therefore sets aside). In short, he thinks that it isn't even a reply to the sceptic because it misunderstands his challenge.

It can look as though the sceptic wants you to decide between competing hypotheses as to whether you meant addition rather than quaddition by 'plus'. But really all talk of quaddition is dispensable; and when it is dispensed with the appeal to simplicity can be seen to miss the point. The question was this: what fact was there in virtue of which you meant addition by 'plus'? It is indeed *a* desideratum on an answer that the fact it points to is *also* one in virtue of which you did *not* mean *quaddition* by 'plus'. But the relative simplicity of addition doesn't point us to *any* fact.

Here is an analogy. It is hard to see how there could be a fact anywhere in the universe in virtue of which Lady Macbeth (the character in the play, not the historical person) had children. Nothing in the play, I suppose, settles the matter either way. I might challenge you to find such a fact. Then it would be a desideratum on your reply that the fact in virtue of which she had children *also* be a fact in virtue of which she was *not* childless. Now you might say that the hypothesis that she had children is the *simpler* hypothesis (let us imagine that it is). But that is no reply to my challenge. It doesn't point to any fact in virtue of which she had children. At most it tells us this: *if* there is a fact either way then it is the fact that she had children. But that was never in dispute. What is at issue is whether there *is* a fact either way.

Similarly, the present reply to the sceptic at most tells us this: if there is a fact as to whether I meant addition or quaddition then I meant addition. But that was never in dispute. The whole issue was whether there *is* a fact either way.

I take all this to be the gist of the discussion at W:38, which seems to me to be decisive.[6]

4.2.3 Introspectible Mental States: The 'Cube' Objection

Perhaps the most intuitively attractive reply to the sceptic is that your meaning addition by 'plus' was an introspectible mental state. There was on this view something like a *feeling* associated with 'plus' and it is this association in virtue of which you meant addition and not quaddition. Let us call this *sensationalism*.

Kripke attacks sensationalism in three ways. He argues that it fails to satisfy INR: no awareness of any such association can *tell* you what to say (W:41–3). He argues that no such association is sufficient for your having meant addition (W:44–6). And he argues that no such association is necessary for your having meant addition (W:46). I consider the first of these objections here and the next two at 4.2.4 and 4.2.5.

Kripke makes two points. Firstly, he thinks it unclear how an introspectible state can tell you what to say when queried about '68 plus 57':

How on earth would this headache help me figure out whether I ought to answer '125' or '5' when asked about '68 + 57'? If I think the headache indicates that I ought to say '125', would there be anything about it to refute a sceptic's contention that, on the contrary, it indicates that I ought to say '5'? (W:42)

Secondly, he thinks that it *is* clear that an introspectible state cannot tell you how to proceed:

> For example (*Philosophical Investigations* 139), a drawing of a cube comes to my mind whenever I hear or say the word 'cube'... 'In what sense can this picture fit or fail to fit the use of the word "cube"? – Perhaps you say "It's quite simple; – if that picture comes to me and I point to a triangular prism, for instance, and say it's a cube, then this use of the word doesn't fit the picture." But doesn't it fit? I have purposely so chosen the example that it is quite easy to imagine a *method of projection* according to which the picture does fit after all. The picture of the cube did indeed *suggest* a certain use to us, but it was possible for me to use it differently.' The sceptic could suggest that the image be used in non-standard ways ... No internal impression, with a *quale*, could possibly tell me in itself how it is to be applied in future cases. (W:42–3)

I agree with the first point but not with the second. The supposed possibility of alternative applications *does* show the following: if introspectible mental states tell you how to apply a word in novel cases then they cannot do so in the way that physical models and tables do. It cannot be the case that one 'looks something up' in a mental image and then interprets it to generate an application of the associated word. To adapt a simile of Descartes: if understanding consists in a sensational state then that state cannot guide you in the way that a pilot is guided by the instruments on his ship.

But have we any other model of how a mental state of meaning guides behaviour? We do: I have in mind the felt location of sensational states like itches, tickles and pains. I feel a pain in my hand. It feels like a pain; but more than that it *feels* like a pain *in my hand*. But what is there about a mere feeling that can so much as tell me where it is: that can so much as guide my attention to one part of space rather than another? Well, it is quite unclear *how* it does this (that is why I agree with Kripke's first point); but it is intuitively clear *that* it does so (that is why I disagree with his second). There is something about the feeling itself that does it. It is quite natural to say that it is a feature of that very sensation itself that *guides* my attention towards my hand, which therefore can itself be said to enter into the intentional content of the pain (Ayers 1993, vol. 1:215). It is equally natural to say that the sensation *tells* me where to direct my attention (if I want to alleviate the pain). The possibility of alternative uses or interpretations, which seemed so compelling in the 'cube' case, just doesn't get a grip in the case of felt pains. If you feel a pain in your hand then there is no 'method of projection' that will justify pointing to your leg instead. Here it seems that we have a sensational state with just the property that Kripke says is impossible: it can tell you 'in itself' how to proceed.

If we can say this about felt pains then why can't we say it about the sensational state supposedly associated with 'plus'? That state *guides* you to the right answer: it *tells* you what to say (if you want to give the right answer). It contains future uses of 'plus' in itself in just the way that a pain in the hand contains a location in itself.

I am not saying that there *is* a content-bearing sensational state associated with 'plus' but only that Kripke's argument doesn't establish its impossibility – though it does generate appropriate puzzlement about its operation.

4.2.4 Introspectible Mental States: The Sufficiency Objection

Kripke believes that any sensational state is such that one can both be in it and yet not mean addition by 'plus'. Hence no such state is sufficient for meaning addition by 'plus'. Kripke gives three arguments for this.

Two of them appear in the following:

> It takes relatively little introspective acuteness to realize the dubiousness of the attribution of a special qualitative character to the 'experience' of meaning addition by 'plus' ... Suppose I perform a particular addition now, say '5 + 7'. Is there any special quality to the experience? Would it have been different if I had been trained in, and performed, the corresponding quaddition? How different indeed would the *experience* have been if I had performed the corresponding multiplication ('5 × 7'), other

than that I would have responded automatically with a different answer? (Try the experiment yourself.) (W:44–5)

One of these arguments concerns multiplication; the other concerns quaddition.

The argument concerning multiplication is that automatically adding five and seven feels just the same as automatically *multiplying* five and seven. The feeling associated with both the automatic addition and the automatic multiplication cannot therefore be sufficient for either.

The argument is valid and probably sound: at any rate my own introspection verifies its premise. But its conclusion has no force against the sensationalist, who could reply as follows. There is an association between 'plus' and a certain sensational state in virtue of which you mean addition by 'plus'. It is therefore true that whenever you have that state in response to '7 + 5', you are adding and not multiplying. But (the sensationalist continues) the state need only appear when your response to the query *draws upon your understanding* of 'plus'. And automatic responses to addition and multiplication problems do not draw upon your understanding of 'plus' and 'times': they are simply vocal reactions to phonetic cues. When I was a child I like many others learnt the multiplication and addition tables for small numbers (less than 12) by heart. I can therefore respond in a correct but parrot-like fashion to small addition and multiplication problems. It is true that no feeling accompanies my response to '7 + 5' that doesn't also accompany my response to '7 × 5'. But that does *not* show that my understanding of 'plus' and 'times' doesn't consist in my associating those words with a certain feeling. It only shows that my *automatic* responses to queries of the form '*x* plus *y*' do *not* draw upon my understanding of 'plus' and 'times' any more than those of a computer. By contrast, cases where my responses are *not* automatic plausibly *do* involve distinctive feelings. It seems plain to me that when asked about '43 × 37' I *do* get a feeling (of 'calculating in the head'); and just as plain that it is a different feeling from what I get when asked about '44 × 36'.

In short: the sensationalist can accept Kripke's conclusion that no feeling is sufficient for *automatic* addition but maintain that some feeling is sufficient for non-automatic addition. It is compatible with his view that some feeling is sufficient for *meaning* addition.

The argument concerning quaddition is immune to this criticism. Its force derives from the fact that for numbers less than 57 the answer to a quaddition is the *same* as the answer to an addition. Hence even if the numbers involved are large enough for us not to be able to give an automatic response it is still introspectively plausible that the feeling that accompanies thoughtful addition (say, '48 plus 36') is the same as the feeling that accompanies the corresponding thoughtful quaddition ('48 quus 36'). So the argument is this: the same feeling accompanies both the addition and the corresponding quaddition. So it is insufficient for meaning either.

The argument is valid; and again my own introspection verifies its premise. But the sensationalist can accept its conclusion so long as he denies that there is *one single* sensation associated with 'plus' in virtue of which you meant addition by it. He can instead say this: it suffices for your having meant addition by 'plus' that you were disposed to have *some* particular feeling in response to each query of the form '*x* plus *y*'. But it need not have been the *same* feeling for every such query. So: when asked about '48 plus 36' you get the feeling F1 that you also get when asked about '48 quus 36'; but when asked about '68 plus 57' you get a feeling F2 that differs from both F1 *and* the feeling F3 that you get when asked about '68 quus 57'. The fact that you get F1 when asked about '48 plus 36' doesn't by itself suffice to rule out your having meant quaddition by 'plus'; but the fact that you were disposed to get F2 and not F3 when asked about '68 plus 57' does suffice to rule it out. In short, Kripke's argument won't work against someone who identifies meaning addition with a disposition to have certain sensational states in response to particular queries.

That a sensationalist theory has to incorporate this 'dispositionalism' was clear all along from the fact that there are far too many shades of green to think of all at once: hence the association of no one sensational state with 'green' could possibly suffice for meaning green by it. Moreover it is just this kind of dispositionalism that appears to have been proposed (for a different reason) by Kripke's declared example (W:63n51) of a sensationalist – Hume:

When we have found a resemblance amongst several objects, that often occur to us, we apply the same name to all of them, whatever differences we may observe in the degrees of their quantity and quality, and whatever other differences may appear among them. After we have acquired a custom of this kind, the hearing of that name revives the idea of one of these objects, and makes the imagination conceive it with all its particular circumstances and proportions. But as the same word is suppos'd to have been frequently applied to other individuals, that are different in many respects from that idea, which is immediately present to the mind; the word not being able to revive the idea of all those individuals, only touches the soul ... and revives that custom, which we have acquir'd by surveying them. They are not really and in fact present to the mind, but only in power; nor do we draw them all out distinctly in the imagination, but keep ourselves in a readiness to survey any of them, as we may be prompted by a present design or necessity. (Hume 1949:I.i.7)

Thus the word 'green' applies to many particular things: so our grasp of 'green' consists not in the annexing of a single mental image to the word 'green' but rather in the disposition to associate one of a range of ideas (ideas of particular green things) according to the circumstances. Similarly no one feeling is associated with 'plus': your meaning addition by it consists rather in your disposition to associate one of a range of feelings with it depending on what numbers you are adding.

In short, the sensationalist can reply to Kripke's argument concerning quaddition that it only shows the following: the range of feelings dispositionally associated with 'plus' *partially* overlaps that associated with 'quus'. But this doesn't show that either disposition is insufficient for meaning.

Kripke's third argument is based on Wittgenstein's discussion of 'reading', by which is meant only the ability to vocalize a string of written-down expressions according to a rule. The argument is as follows:

Again (*Philosophical Investigations* 160), someone may, under the influence of a drug, or in a dream, be presented with a made-up 'alphabet' and utter certain words, with all the characteristic 'feeling' of reading, to the extent that such a 'feeling' exists at all. If, after the drug wears off (or he wakes up), he himself thinks he was uttering words at random with no real connection with the script, should we really say he was reading? (W:46)

Applied to 'plus' the argument is this. Suppose some drugged patient A was asked a series of questions of the form 'x plus y' and gave a sequence of answers with every feeling of 'adding'. After the drug wears off he is confident that the answers were random. In that case the natural thing to say (according to Kripke) is that in his drugged state he didn't really mean addition. So the feeling is insufficient for the meaning.

But is it really plausible that A didn't mean addition by plus? Imagine being asked about '48 plus 36' under the influence of the drug. You have every feeling of calculating in your head just as you normally do: but you don't *say* '84'; instead you say e.g. '5'. Now wouldn't a more accurate description of your state at the time be, not that you didn't mean addition, but that you did mean it, only for some reason the *words* came out wrong? So why can we not say the same about A: he *did* mean addition but the words came out wrong? A's position while under the influence of the drug is like that of the absent-minded man who at the order 'Right turn!' turns left. It isn't as though he *didn't* understand 'right' to mean right. He did – only for some reason he failed to *turn* right. This seems to me at least as natural a description of the situation as Kripke's.

Of course it is true that our ordinary third-person (or A's *ex post facto*) judgements, based as they are only on his random *behaviour* in the drugged state, will be that he did *not* mean anything. And the interpretation I am suggesting would be ruled out if we assumed that the third-person or *post facto* judgements carry greater authority than did A's own judgements at the time. But that assumption begs the question against the sensationalist: from his perspective you are better placed at time t than others at that time or oneself at a later time to say what you now mean by 'plus' because that is when you are best placed to know what your feelings are at t.

I conclude that of Kripke's three arguments only the second (concerning quaddition) has any force. And even that argument has no force against the dispositionalist theory that was (a) held by the most important classical sensationalist and (b) was in any case the most plausible version all along.

4.2.5 Introspectible Mental States: The Necessity Objection

Let us now ask whether an associated feeling is necessary for meaning addition by 'plus'. Kripke's argument against this is brisk and follows on immediately from the discussion of 'reading' upon which it also draws:

> Or, on the other hand, what if the drug leads him to read fluently from a genuine text, but with the 'sensation' of reciting something learned by heart? Wasn't he still reading? (W:46)

Applied to 'plus' the argument is this. Someone could competently add numbers under the influence of a drug without having any of the feelings that accompany ordinary calculations. Isn't he still adding? If so, the feeling of meaning addition by 'plus' cannot be necessary for doing so.

But is it so clear that he *is* adding? There is certainly an intuitive pull towards saying so. But we can explain the intuition as follows: somebody who behaves in this way will of course look to another *just as if* he is adding: so a third person will have as good grounds as he can ever get for saying that he is adding. But the sensationalist might say that we have confused the intuition that he *looks as though* he is adding with the intuition that he *is* adding.

There is in any case an opposing intuition. This person differs in no essential respect from a robot that gives the right answers *without any feelings at all*. So if we say that the man is really adding then should we not say the same about the robot? And though philosophical sophisticates might 'intuit' that the robot is indeed adding, our pre-philosophical intuitions are quite the opposite (Ayers 1993, vol. 1: 280–1). Nor is it clear that the patient would say of himself that he was adding. It would appear to him as though his vocal cords were reciting answers to addition problems in a parrot-like fashion that in no way exploited his conscious understanding of 'plus'. It is quite hard to imagine the situation. In so far as I can make any judgement I think I'd say that *I* wasn't adding but somehow my mouth was coming out with the right answers. The only thing we can conclude with any firmness is that intuition is in this case equivocal.

A distinct argument of Wittgenstein's doesn't involve dubious thought-experiments concerning drugged patients but only attention to what actually happens:

I might have used other words [other than 'feeling the influence'] to hit off the experience I have when I read a word. Thus I might say that the written word *intimates* the sound to me. – Or again, that when one reads, letter and sound form a unity – as it were an alloy ... But now just read a few sentences in print as you usually do when you are not thinking about the concept of reading; and ask yourself whether you had such experiences of unity, of being influenced and the rest, as you read. – Don't say you had them unconsciously! Nor should we be misled by the picture which suggests that these phenomena came in sight 'on closer inspection'. If I am supposed to describe how an object looks from far off, I don't make the description more accurate by saying what can be noticed about the object on closer inspection. (1967: section 171)

The implication is that you didn't have those experiences in the ordinary course of reading (or adding) because you weren't aware of them. When you focus your attention on reading you seem to have them. But that doesn't mean they were there all along.

But doesn't it? It can often happen that one *has* experiences without *noticing* them, without their being so to speak at the forefront of one's mind. *We* sometimes have experiences in the way Descartes thought animals *always* have them, who 'do not see as we do when we are aware that we see, but only as we do when our mind is elsewhere' (1984–1991, vol.3: 61–2). If you are sitting down, focus on the feeling of pressure caused by the chair in your back. Haven't you been having that feeling for as long as you've been sitting down? You had not noticed it until now: but we do not want to say that it wasn't there all along. After all, it isn't as though you felt no pressure and then suddenly began to feel it when you directed your attention to it (that too is possible but it would feel quite different). Here it seems that *nothing* is misleading about the 'picture which suggests that these phenomena came into sight "on closer inspection"'. Why then is it misleading in the case of reading or adding? Why could it not be that when one focuses on the activity reading one becomes aware of feelings that were there all along? The matter clearly deserves extended discussion. All I will say for the moment is that *Philosophical Investigations* section 171 is hardly a knockdown refutation of sensationalism.

Let me conclude this section by summarizing the gist of it and the previous two. We saw an argument that sensational states cannot tell me to say '125' when queried about '68 plus 57'. We saw three arguments that no such state is sufficient for meaning addition. And we saw two arguments (one from Kripke, one from Wittgenstein) that no such state is necessary. I have argued that five of these arguments are inconclusive against any form of sensationalism, and one of them (the second argument for insufficiency) is impotent against the dispositionalist version attributed to Hume, which therefore survives all six objections. The Humean theory does however involve appeal to dispositions as well as to sensations, and Kripke has independent arguments against a dispositional theory. We consider these at 4.3.

Recall finally that at 4.2.1 I said that one version of the 'rule-assimilation' theory was that meaning consists in an introspectible mental state. Kripke's arguments against that position therefore rely on his arguments against sensationalism. Since his arguments against the latter are inconclusive so too are his arguments against the former.[7]

4.2.6 Sui Generis States

Although Kripke ultimately denies the view that meaning addition is an introspectible mental state he does have some sympathy with its motivation. This is the idea that the sceptic is wrong to seek a reduction of meaning-facts, i.e. a description of them in other terms. Sensationalism is anti-reductionist because it identifies meaning with something that is itself irreducible (W:41).

Even if we reject sensationalism, we can hold on to the view that the sceptic is wrong to look for a reduction:

> Perhaps we may try to recoup, by arguing that meaning addition by 'plus' is a state even more *sui generis* than we have argued before. Perhaps it is simply a primitive state, not to be assimilated to sensations or headaches or any 'qualitative' states, nor to be assimilated to dispositions, but a state of a unique kind of its own. (W:51)

Kripke has two arguments against this position: an epistemological one and a logical one.

The epistemological argument is that a *sui generis* state would fail to meet the fundamental normativity requirement INR, the requirement that awareness of a putative fact about meaning should *tell* you what to say in response to '68 plus 57' (see 4.1.3). This requirement has two consequences: (i) that anybody who was aware of the meaning-fact should be guided to say '125' and not '5'; (ii) that you are in fact aware of the putative-meaning fact and that it does in fact guide you to say '125' and not '5'. Kripke's point is that consequence (ii) doesn't apply here.[8]

> It is not supposed to be an introspectible state, yet we supposedly are aware of it with some fair degree of certainty whenever it occurs. For how else can each of us be confident that he *does*, at present, mean addition by 'plus'? (W:51)

Now you might object that: (i) you can know your mental states without introspection; (ii) the fact that a state has no distinctive phenomenology doesn't imply that it isn't introspectible (see Boghossian 1989:179, 186 for both objections; see McGinn 1984:89 for the second).

In response to (i): it may be true that your belief e.g. that you are thinking about water, qualifies as knowledge despite not being based on introspection. It may be e.g. that the belief qualifies as knowledge because the object of the (second-order) belief is constitutively that of the content of the (first-order) thought, so that if e.g. you believe that you are thinking about water then it cannot but be the case that you are thinking about water (Burge 1988).

But this account of first-person authority if applied to meaning-facts makes it quite unclear how awareness of them can guide your action. Imagine the following. On Monday you meant addition by 'plus' but on Tuesday you suddenly started meaning *quaddition* by it. At noon on Monday you are asked about '68 plus 57' and you answer '125'. At noon on Tuesday you are asked the same question and you answer '5'. Now let it be true that you believe all day on Monday that you mean addition and on Tuesday that you mean quaddition; let it also be true that these second-order beliefs both qualify as knowledge. (The difference between the contents of the beliefs, and their amounting to knowledge, both follow from the fact that the two *sui generis* states in question themselves enter into your beliefs about what you mean.) It is *still* true, if meanings are *not* introspectible, that your state on Monday morning and your state on Tuesday morning are indiscernible. It follows that there is no discernible feature of your state on Tuesday that *guides* you to say '5' rather than '125' in response to '68 plus 57'. But that just means that the *sui generis* view still fails to satisfy INR. For, even when it is supplemented with a non-introspection-based account of your knowledge that you mean quaddition, it still makes no room for the basic idea that what you mean is something awareness of which is supposed to guide your future responses.

In short: (i) misses the point of INR. The difficulty with the *sui generis* proposal isn't so much (a) that it entails that you cannot know that you mean addition by 'plus' when you do, but rather (b) that it entails that your meaning addition by 'plus' is indiscernible from your meaning *quaddition* by it. The proposed reply (i) is that (a) is false; but since according to it what you mean isn't introspectible, (b) is still true. And it isn't because of (a) but because of (b) that the *sui generis* proposal fails to satisfy INR.

As for (ii): it is actually quite unclear *how* one might be able to have introspective knowledge of a state that possesses no distinctive phenomenology. Boghossian's example is aspect-perception. We see the famous drawing (Wittgenstein 1967:194) now as a duck, now as a rabbit:

> But this change of 'aspect', although manifestly introspectible, is nevertheless not a change in something qualitative, for the qualitative character of the visual experience remains the same even as the aspect changes. (Boghossian 1989:179n61)

The passage is highly suggestive: perhaps meaning addition rather than quaddition could be said to consist in seeing certain examples under one aspect rather than another. But to speak for myself, I find it hard to deny that aspect-perception does possess a distinctive phenomenology. It would indeed be misleading to call a change in aspect a change in the *visual* experience: when asked to draw what I see I will draw the same whether I am seeing it as a duck or as a rabbit (Wittgenstein 1967:196). But still there is such a thing as *what it feels like* to notice a change in aspect. Or if there is not, I am not sure what content there can be to the claim that one's belief that one sees it as a duck isn't just authoritative but genuinely *introspective*.

Now it might be alleged that facts about other mental states such as desires, intentions, memories, etc. face the same problem: it seems that we have introspective knowledge of them, and yet it isn't clear how we can have this knowledge if indeed they have no phenomenological correlate (see 3.4.1(ii)). But this observation generalizes rather than alleviates the trouble. Hume's inability to find his *self* in occurrent consciousness dealt a devastating blow to the Cartesian claim of introspectible knowledge of it. Why then should the fact that beliefs and desires are (as Wright says) 'fugitive to occurrent consciousness' not do similar damage to the idea that we have privileged introspective access to *them*?[9]

So I think Kripke's epistemological argument is effective.

The *logical* argument runs as follows:

> Such a state would have to be a finite object, contained in our finite minds. It does not consist in my explicitly thinking of each case of the addition table, nor even of my encoding each separate case in the brain: we lack the capacity for that ... Can we conceive of a finite state which *could* not be interpreted in a quus-like way? How could that be? (W:52)

There are three things to note about this argument.

Firstly, Kripke is granting for its sake what the epistemological argument disputed, namely that the alleged *sui generis* state of meaning addition is something of which somebody who is in it might be directly aware. The objection is that even if you *were* aware of the state you could interpret it in a quus-like way. So understood, the argument is that such a state fails to satisfy consequence (i) of INR: awareness of such a state doesn't preclude quus-like applications of it. As such the argument is as decisive as the 'cube' argument against sensationalism considered at 4.2.3: if you accept that argument then you ought also to grant this one.

Secondly, if the logical argument is interpreted like this then Kripke's play with 'finitude' is unnecessary (as he is aware: W: 52n34). Even if you did possess an *infinitary* state, it too could be interpreted in a non-standard way (i.e. in a grue-like rather than a quus-like way: see 4.1.2 and W:20).

Thirdly, *if* we drop the internal normativity requirement as an axiom about meaning, the objection has little force. Suppose we denied that 'meaning addition by "plus"' refers to an object of awareness and thought of it instead as a *theoretical* term. Meaning is then not something that we 'come across' directly in experience. We should rather think of it the way we actually think of electrical current: it is something that we postulate as part of a theoretical explanation of what we *do* observe. It might seem mysterious how facts about current can entail infinitely many distinct facts about resistance and voltage. But it isn't mysterious at all: current is *just the sort of thing* referred to by the term 'I' in a certain theory one of whose theorems is Ohm's law that $V = I.R$. And this has infinitely many consequences (e.g. that if the current is 5 Amps and the resistance is 2 Ohms then the voltage is 10 Volts). The reason we believe that there is such a thing is that that theory forms together with ancillary theories (concerning the behaviour of voltmeters, etc.) part of a systematic explanation of what we observe. Similarly, meaning addition by 'plus' is *just the sort of thing* referred to by a term that forms part of a theory of human behaviour: it may be a theorem of that theory that anybody who means addition, who believes that he has been queried about '68 plus 57', who desires to give the right answer and who doesn't miscalculate, will answer '125'.[10] We have reason to believe that there is such a thing in so far as the meaning-attribution helps to explain behaviour, in particular the writing down and uttering of certain numerals. And the postulation that somebody means addition by 'plus' will of course have infinitely many consequences for that person's behaviour under various circumstances in the same manner as the postulation of a particular current. In short, the apparently mysterious fecundity of the *sui generis* meaning-fact is not mysterious at all: it derives from the logical fecundity of the theory in which 'meaning' is embedded.

To summarize: if a *sui generis* mental state is not an object of awareness then the view that its past existence constituted your having meant addition is vulnerable to the epistemological argument, provided always that we assume INR. If it is an object of awareness then the logical argument is as effective as the argument against meaning-states being introspectible mental states, provided always that we assume INR. But if we do *not* assume INR then neither argument works.

4.2.7 Meanings as Platonic Entities

The reader will recall (2.1.3(ii)) that Frege thought that names have a sense that determines what they refer to. The sense is grasped by anyone who understands the term and it settles the correct application of the term. One might take the same view of 'plus' as was there taken of proper names: it too has a sense that determines its correct application.

Now the sense of an expression isn't in any way contained 'within my mind', at least not if that means that it is *only* contained there. The sense of a term is non-subjective in that numerically distinct persons can grasp numerically the same sense. That requirement, Frege thought, was necessary for science to be a common possession (1956: 301–2). In fact he thought that sense is wholly objective: it would exist just as it was even if there were no people to have any thoughts at all. As well as being objective it is, he thought, abstract: it has neither causal powers nor location (1956: 307ff.). It is what we nowadays call a 'Platonic' object.

Now can't it be the *sense* attached to 'plus' in virtue of which you meant addition by it? Two abstract entities are relevant here: the sense of addition and the sense of quaddition. The suggestion is that you meant addition through having somehow connected the former rather than the latter with 'plus'.

The objectivity of sense means there is no difficulty in saying that the sense of addition is infinite. So there is no problem in saying that *it* encodes the answer to *every* addition problem: and this distinguishes it from quaddition.

This is all very well as far as it goes but it doesn't go far enough. The account does not explain how it is that a *person* can mean addition rather than quaddition by 'plus'. You have only added (or quadded) numbers less than 57. So what is there about you in virtue of which you connect 'plus' with the addition-sense rather than the admittedly distinct quaddition-sense? This isn't to say that the account is false but only that so far it has not answered the sceptic. What we need in addition is some account of how *we non*-Platonic persons can be made aware of, and hence guided by, Platonic entities (Zalabardo 2003: 315). The objection is again that Platonic entities fail to satisfy INR.

That is the gist of Kripke's very brief discussion (W:53–4). I think he is quite right to regard Platonism as unsatisfactory.

4.2.8 Conclusion

We saw Kripke's arguments against five responses to the sceptic:

(1) That meaning addition by 'plus' consists in assimilation of a rule

(2) That it consists in the simplicity of the addition function
(3) That it consists in an introspectible mental state
(4) That it is *sui generis*
(5) That it consists in the connection of 'plus' with a Platonic entity

He argued decisively against (2) and (5). The argument against (1) is decisive if 'assimilation of a rule' means awareness of some verbalization of the rule. His argument against (4) is decisive if (4) entails that the state in question isn't an object of direct awareness. But (1) could instead be understood as identical with (3), i.e. the view that meaning is an introspectible mental state. In that case Kripke's case against it is no stronger than his arguments against (3). And we saw that one version of (3) survives Kripke's criticisms: the view that your having meant addition consisted in a disposition to be in one of a range of mental states, awareness of which guided your answer to particular problems of the form '*x* plus *y*'.

4.3 DISPOSITIONALISM

We saw that up to now you have neither added nor quadded numbers greater than 56; and yet it seems intuitive that you meant addition all along. What made this true? The question sounds a little bit like this one: you believed all your life that the Earth is more than 28 days old but you have never said or probably even consciously thought that it was. So what made it true that you *did* believe it? This is a natural answer: if you *had* been asked whether the Earth was more than 28 days old you *would* have said yes. This fact doesn't concern your *actual* past behaviour but only your past *dispositions*. The parallel response to the sceptic is as follows:

> To mean addition by ' + ' is to be disposed, when asked for any sum '*x* + *y*' to give the sum of *x* and *y* as the answer (in particular, to say '125' when queried about '68 + 57'); to mean quus is to be disposed when queried about any arguments, to respond with their *quum* (in particular to answer '5' when queried about '68 + 57') ... To say that in fact I meant plus in the past is to say – as surely was the case! – that had I been queried about '68 + 57', I *would* have answered '125'. By hypothesis I was not in fact asked, but the disposition was present none the less. (W:22–3)

Kripke raises the following objections to dispositionalism: it doesn't satisfy INR (23–4); my dispositions are finite (26–7); we are disposed to make mistakes (28–32). The material immediately following these objections (33–7) applies them to the theory of the 'machine as symbol', generalizes them and summarizes them. I shall not discuss this but only Kripke's three objections to dispositionalism.

4.3.1 Dispositions and Justification

Kripke's first objection is that dispositionalism isn't really an answer at all: it doesn't exhibit any fact that justifies your presently answering '125' rather than '5' when faced with '68 plus 57'.

> To a good extent this reply immediately ought to appear to be misdirected, off target ... How does it *justify* my choice of '125'? What it says is: ' "125" is the response that you are disposed to give, and (perhaps the reply adds) it would also have been your response in the past.' Well and good, I know that '125' is the response I am disposed to give (I am actually giving it!), and maybe it is helpful to be told – as a matter of brute fact – that I would have given the same answer in the past. How does any of this indicate that – now *or* in the past – '125' was an answer *justified* in terms of instructions I gave myself, rather than a mere jack-in-the-box unjustified and arbitrary response? (W:23)

He then considers two possible responses. The first is that my present response of '125' might be justified by my *past* disposition to answer '125'. He criticizes it as follows:

> Am I supposed to justify my present belief that I meant addition, not quaddition, and hence should answer '125', in terms of a *hypothesis* about my *past* dispositions? (Do I record and investigate the past physiology of my brain?) Why am I so sure that one particular hypothesis of this kind is correct, when all my past thoughts can be construed either so that I meant plus or so that I meant quus? (W:23)

The second is that my present response of '125' is justified by my *present* disposition so to respond. He criticizes this as follows:

Alternatively, is the hypothesis to refer to my present disposition alone, which would hence give the right answer by definition? Nothing is more contrary to our ordinary view – or Wittgenstein's – than is the supposition that 'whatever is going to seem right to me is right.' (1967: section 258). On the contrary, 'that only means that here we can't talk about right' (*ibid.*). (W:23–24)

Let us consider these two points in order.

Kripke's criticism of the idea that my present response is justified by my past dispositions might itself be criticized. One might say that your past dispositions *do* justify present responses that are in accordance with them, because you *ought* to use words in a way that is *consistent* with your past dispositions to use them. Otherwise communication (either with others or your own later self) would be impossible (Coates 1986: 78).

But this misunderstands what kind of justification Kripke has in mind. There is of course *a* common sense of 'justification' on which an action or an actor can be justified by something that they need *not* be aware of, as when St Paul says 'It is God that justifieth'. An action might be justified in this sense by some unforeseen and beneficial consequence of it. And it may be that in this sense the consistency of your present response with your past dispositions justifies the former.

But Kripke is applying a more 'internal' sense of justification. In this sense one's actions are justified only by what you are *aware* of and *in the light of which* you act. (That is the content of INR.) Now even though you were in the past disposed to say '125' and not '5', that cannot in *this* sense justify your doing so. The sceptic was at pains to point out that you are *in fact* unaware of anything about your past in virtue of which you had that disposition. Such a fact may indeed have obtained: but it cannot be what justifies your present response. That is the point of the parenthetical and rhetorical question about the past state of your brain. Even if there were neurophysiological facts that disposed you to say '125', you are not presently aware of them, so it cannot be your awareness of *them* that guides you to '125'. In short, facts about your past dispositions fail to meet INR; hence they cannot be the facts in virtue of which you meant addition. (Note also that without INR the parenthetical question makes no sense.)

Now consider the idea that your *present* disposition justifies your present response. A dispositionalist who thinks that might deny that 'whatever is going to seem right to me is right'. He might e.g. distinguish between the mechanisms that jointly determine your disposition. Some of these mechanisms (in virtue of which you meant addition) by themselves dispose you to say '125'; but this need not mean that you are in fact going to say '125', because there might be interfering mechanisms which together with the 'legitimate' ones yield a net disposition to say e.g. '124'. Then the dispositionalist might maintain that saying '125' is justified by your 'legitimate' dispositions: and there is no guarantee that *whatever* you end up saying is so justified because what you say might be in part the upshot of 'interfering' mechanisms. (Goldfarb 1985: 98)

But Kripke's response to this will be the same as before. It may be that the distinction between meaning-dispositions and interfering mechanisms leaves room for some responses to be justified and others unjustified in the *Pauline* sense. But the distinction isn't available to consciousness: it cannot therefore be in *its* light that you are guided to say '125'.[11] Hence this version of dispositionalism again fails to satisfy INR and must be rejected.

Note finally that neither objection considered here has any force against the dispositionalist sensationalism attributed at 4.2.4 to Hume. Both objections are that one's (past or present) dispositions to *respond* cannot themselves justify those responses. But for Hume it is not dispositions to *respond* that constitute your meaning addition: it is dispositions to have certain *ideas*. The Humean can maintain that one's present responses *are* 'internally' justified by the feelings that one is presently disposed to have when calculating '68 plus 57'. This view certainly makes room for distinguishing what you do from what you ought to be doing. For the feelings that justify an action might (if e.g. the subject is absent-minded) in fact fail to produce it.

In short: both of Kripke's 'justification' objections are effective against their target versions of dispositionalism if, but only if, we assume INR. But they are ineffective against dispositional sensationalism in either case.

4.3.2 The Finitude Objection

We saw at 4.1.1 that it was sufficient for the sceptical problem to arise that you have in the past made only a finite number of *actual* responses. Kripke objects to the dispositionalist that there are also only finitely many *counterfactual* responses that you would make. So it cannot be in virtue of your past dispositions that you meant addition by 'plus':

> It is not true, for example, that if queried about the sum of any two numbers, no matter how large, I will reply with their actual sum, for some pairs of numbers are simply too large for my mind – or my brain – to grasp. (W:26–7)

One might then modify dispositionalism as follows. What you mean by 'plus' isn't determined by the responses that you would *in fact* give but rather by those that you would give *if you had the capacity*. If, for example,

> my brain had been stuffed with sufficient extra matter to grasp large enough numbers, and if it were given enough capacity to perform such a large addition, and if my life (in a healthy state) were prolonged enough, then given an addition problem involving two large numbers, m and n, I would respond with their sum, and not with the result according to some quus-like rule. (W:27)

This version of dispositionalism seems to get around the objection.

But Kripke objects that it is either vacuous or circular. Clearly 'extra mental capacity' needs to be more carefully specified. If e.g. your mind or brain were augmented with material that disposed you to *quadd* rather than to *add* numbers greater than 56 you would respond '5' rather than '125' to the query '68 plus 57'. So the proposal needs to be something like this: what made it true that you meant addition in the past was the fact that if your brain had been augmented with the disposition to *add* large numbers then you would respond with their sum. But that cannot suffice for your actually having meant addition, for it is equally true that if your brain had been augmented with the disposition to *quadd* large numbers then you would respond with their quum. Of course what is really wanted is this: if your mind were augmented with the disposition to *carry out your past intentions* with respect to large numbers you would respond with their sum and not their quum. But the circularity of that proposal is evident (W:28): for what was there in virtue of which you intended all along to *add* rather than to *quadd*?

Here is an analogy. My calculator can add numbers less than 57 but breaks down for bigger numbers. You and I are disputing whether it is an adding or a quadding device. You say it is an adding device on the grounds that if you expanded its circuitry in a suitable way it would if queried about '68 + 57' give the answer '125'. But I respond quite reasonably that this undisputed fact cannot suffice for its being an adding device. For it is also true that if the calculator's circuitry were expanded in *some* suitable way then it would instead give the answer '5'. And now how can you say without begging the question that the first expansion is 'suitable' but the second is not?

But maybe there *is* a non-question-begging way to specify a 'suitable' expansion of my brain. We might say this: if you had been granted extra *memory* and extra *longevity* then you would have responded with the sum and not the quum when asked to add large numbers. This way of specifying the augmentation begs no questions, for it doesn't assume from the outset that what is to be augmented is your adding rather than your quadding abilities. It says only that if you had been granted extra capacities that would be necessary for the better computing of *any* binary function, you would amongst other things have responded to '*x* plus *y*' with their sum and not their quum. (Fodor 1990: 94–5. For criticism see Kusch 2006:101–5.)

In any case, even if we concede that the finitude objection is effective, it is not clear that it generalizes to the wholesale meaning-scepticism advertised at 4.1.2 (see W:22). It does *not* show that there are for the dispositionalist *no facts about meaning at all*. It only shows that there are no facts in virtue of which you meant one *infinitary* function rather than another. But it is still a fact that one means by 'plus' a function other than quaddition in the original sense of the latter. Facts about meaning would then involve an indeterminacy rather like that of visual images. You can visualize a tiger: it is then a fact that you visualize a tiger, not a monkey. But there may be no fact about the number of its stripes (Fodor 1975: vol. 2, 77–8). This doesn't mean that there are *no* facts about visualization but only that they give out at a certain level of detail. Similarly, the dispositionalist might dispute the sceptical claim that there are no facts about what you meant by 'plus' while conceding that there is no fact that you meant *addition* by it. But this means only that the facts about what you mean give out at a certain level of detail. The dispositionalist who takes this line may have to abandon the idea (proposed by Miller 2000: 164) that any facts underpinning meaning would have to rule out your meaning at least one of any pair of non-co-extensional functions. But he could still retain the dispositionalist thesis that a change of meaning implies a change in underlying dispositions (Horwich 1995: 363). This concessionary dispositionalism is certainly highly revisionary of our ordinary beliefs about meaning. But it does less violence to them than scepticism. So maybe it is preferable to the latter.

In short, Kripke's finitude objection is ineffective for two reasons. Firstly: the dispositionalist can appeal to idealizations about memory, longevity, etc. without obviously begging the question. Secondly: even if the objection is granted, this doesn't show that dispositions are *not* facts about meaning but only that they do not determine what function is meant up to a unique extension.

Note finally that both replies are also available to the dispositionalist version of sensationalism. The proponent of that theory can refine it by appealing to idealizations regarding memory, or he can concede that dispositions to have particular feelings do not specify what you meant up to a unique extension while maintaining that they are facts about what you meant. So he need fear nothing from the finitude objection.

4.3.3 The Mistakes Objection

If what you meant was determined by what you would have said then it seems inevitable that many people cannot mean addition by 'plus' because they would have made mistakes. Kripke sees in this fact a potent objection to dispositionalism:

> Most of us have dispositions to make mistakes. For example, when asked to add certain numbers some people forget to 'carry'. They are thus disposed, for these numbers, to give an answer differing from the usual addition table ... In the present instance a certain unique function (call it 'skaddition') corresponds in its table exactly to the subject's dispositions, including his dispositions to make mistakes. (Waive the difficulty that the subject's dispositions are finite: suppose he has a disposition to respond to any pair of arguments.) So, where common sense

holds that the subject means the same addition function as everyone else but systematically makes computational mistakes, the dispositionalist seems forced to hold that the subject makes no computational mistakes, but means a non-standard function ('skaddition') by ' + '. (W:28–30)

Suppose you have the disposition to forget to carry the 1 when adding 484 to 516. So you would have responded '990' rather than '1000' had you been queried about '484 + 516'. Let skaddition be the function # that is exactly like addition except that if you skadd 484 and 516 then you get 990. Then the dispositionalist appears to be saying falsely that you meant skaddition and not addition by ' + '.

The obvious reply is to distinguish between (a) the answer you were immediately disposed to give and (b) the answer that you would have given *on reflection*. A modified dispositionalism would say that it is (b) and not (a) that determines what you meant by ' + '; this theory allows for mistakes because (a) and (b) might diverge (Blackburn 1984: 36). To see how (b) applies to skaddition: that function isn't associative. The value of 1#(484#516) is distinct from that of (1#484)#516. But you believed that ' + ' denotes an associative function. So you would on reflection have withdrawn your answer '990' to '484 + 516' and probably eventually come up with '1000' instead. That is why you were not skadding but adding all along.

Kripke doesn't explicitly discuss this. But he considers and dismisses the similar proposal that what you meant is determined by what you would have said upon correction by *others*. He writes:

One cannot repair matters by urging that the subject would eventually respond with the right answer after correction by others. First, there are uneducable subjects who will persist in their error even after persistent correction. Second, what is meant by 'correction by others'? If it means rejection by others of 'wrong' answers ... and suggestion of the 'right' answer ... then again the account is circular. If random intervention is allowed ... then, although educable subjects may be induced to correct their wrong answers, suggestible subjects may also be induced to replace their correct answers with erroneous ones. (W:32)

This reply to 'communal' dispositionalism suggests a parallel response to the individualistic dispositionalist who appeals to (b)-type dispositions. Presumably Kripke would say: some subjects are uneducable by reflection; even after lengthy reflection they would persist in answering '990' to '484 + 516'. Other subjects may be *too* educable by reflection: it might lead them to settle on no answer (Kusch 2006: 113). The dispositionalist must say that these persons would not mean addition by ' + '.

But is this so hard to swallow? If after repeated checking of your calculation (or if you like repeated correction by others) you persisted in saying '990', is there really any harm in saying that you *did* mean skaddition? There are certainly cases where your *immediate* disposition in propitious circumstances to diverge from standard use intuitively implies divergence from standard meaning (e.g. direct applications of 'green' – Coates 1997: 16). Why then should we not infer a divergence in meaning from *persistent* recalcitrance of this sort? There is usually no clear place for a third party to draw the line between persistent, inexplicable disagreement and divergence in meaning. It is in particular unclear why we should insist that someone who persists with '990' really means addition and not skaddition by ' + '. So it is not a decisive objection to dispositionalism that it says of our maverick adder that he is really a skadder.

In short, the mistakes objection appears to be answerable. Note also that it doesn't arise against sensationalist dispositionalism. Someone who held that view would not in any case identify what one meant with what one was disposed to *say* but rather with the disposition to have a *feeling that guided him* to say it; so for him the fact that one often makes mistakes does not imply that one did not by 'plus' mean addition all along.

4.3.4 Conclusion
So there are three arguments against dispositionalism: the argument from INR, the argument from finitude, and the argument from mistakes. The first of these is effective but the second and third are not. This however suffices to refute dispositionalism provided always that we retain INR.

On the other hand none of the three arguments is effective against the Humean position: dispositional sensationalism. That view must therefore be allowed to survive: for all that *Kripke* has said it remains a possible response to the sceptic.

4.4 SUMMARY

We have now completed our survey of the sceptic's arguments. They aimed to show that there was no fact in virtue of which you meant addition by 'plus'. We considered 14 arguments:

(1) Meaning addition did not consist in assimilation of rules because the statement of the rule fails to satisfy INR (4.2.1)
(2) It did not consist in the simplicity of addition: that misses the sceptic's whole point (4.2.2)
(3) It was not an introspectible mental state because no such state meets INR: the 'cube' argument (4.2.3)
(4) It was not an introspectible mental state because no such state is sufficient: the multiplication argument (4.2.4)
(5) It was not an introspectible mental state because no such state is sufficient: the quaddition argument (4.2.4)
(6) It was not an introspectible mental state because no such state is sufficient: the reading argument (4.2.4)
(7) It was not an introspectible mental state because no such state is necessary: the 'drug' argument (4.2.5)
(8) It was not an introspectible mental state because no such state is necessary: Wittgenstein's argument (4.2.5)
(9) It was not *sui generis* because no such state satisfies INR: the epistemological argument (4.2.6)
(10) It was not *sui generis* because no such state has the right consequences (4.2.6)
(11) It was not a Platonic entity because no such entity satisfies INR (4.2.7)
(12) It was not a disposition because no disposition satisfies INR (4.3.1)
(13) It was not a disposition because dispositions are finite (4.3.2)
(14) It was not a disposition because we are disposed to make mistakes (4.3.3)

I have endorsed (1), (2), (9), (11) and (12) and raised doubts about the others. This is however enough to knock out all the proposed theories except for the hybrid sensational-dispositionalist view

(4.2.4). Anyone who accepts INR but rejects sensationalism should find Kripke's arguments convincing.

I conclude with a brief diagnosis. There are two intuitive thoughts about meaning. The first is that meaning is something that is *revealed* in public use: that is why we find it natural to say that somebody who competently performs sums is really adding, whatever his feelings are at the time. But the second is that meaning antecedently *guides* your use: that is the source of INR. These two thoughts are however in tension (Wright 1989b: 177). The sceptic exploits that tension, arguing first from one direction and then from the other that no fact can satisfy both intuitions. For example: argument (7) exploits the first intuition against sensationalism; argument (12) exploits the second intuition against dispositionalism. Now one might say that Kripke is operating with a notion of meaning into which he has built inconsistent elements: so it is hardly surprising that nothing in reality answers to it. That would be unfair. The tension was there all along in our pre-philosophical concept of meaning: the sceptic's achievement was to bring it to light.

5

PRIVATE LANGUAGE

The arguments so far aimed at showing that there is no fact in virtue of which you meant addition by 'plus'. I stated grounds for doubting some of these arguments: but suppose that they *do* work. Then there *was* no fact in virtue of which you meant addition by 'plus'. Suppose also that they generalize in the way described at 4.1.2. Then there is no fact in virtue of which *anybody* could *ever* mean *anything* by *any* word. That is the sceptical conclusion (W: 69).

At this point it therefore seems surprising that Kripke advertises an argument against a *particular* language, i.e. 'private' language. Doesn't the sceptical argument show that no kind of language can exist? Deploying the argument against private language would be like using a sledgehammer to crack a nut.

In fact Kripke is not proceeding like that. He is not applying the sceptical argument directly against the possibility of private language. His strategy is rather to rehabilitate the notion of meaning in a way that evades the sceptical argument and then to show that the rehabilitated notion only applies to a *public* language (W:60–2). That is: the sceptical arguments do not show that we cannot talk about meaning at all. They only show that meaning-ascriptions require a particular context that excludes the private use of words. All of this will become clearer when we look at the details of the argument of W Chapter 3.

The plan of the chapter is as follows. In 5.1 I describe Kripke's general distinction between 'straight' and 'sceptical' responses to the sceptic (W:62–78) and consider in outline how it is supposed to apply to the case at hand. In 5.2 I consider the details of his 'sceptical solution' (W:86–95). Finally at 5.3 I consider the consequent argument against private language that is intertwined with this solution (W:86–104).

5.1 OUTLINE OF THE SCEPTICAL SOLUTION

Kripke's argument in Chapter 3 seems initially to admit that there are no facts about meaning at all. But he insists that a sceptical reply to the sceptic is none the less available. This reply shows how, even if we grant the sceptic's conclusion, it is still proper to speak of somebody's meaning addition. This is because statements about meaning can themselves be meaningful even if no facts are around to make them true or false. But then where does their meaningfulness come from? It comes from the conditions under which we assert them, and the role that they play in our lives.

At 5.1.1 I describe the distinction between straight and sceptical solutions. At 5.1.2 I outline the rough picture of meaning that enables Kripke to apply a sceptical solution in the present case. At 5.1.3 I consider the intended scope of that picture and whether its application to the present case is coherent.

5.1.1 The Straight Solution and the Sceptical Solution

Scepticism is usually an *epistemological* doctrine: it states that we do not have knowledge of certain alleged truths. Descartes presented (but clearly did not endorse) an argument for this sort of scepticism with regard to the nature of the external world; Hume presented (but did not clearly endorse) sceptical arguments with regard to both the external world and the future course of experience. But the present scepticism is not epistemological but *metaphysical*. It addresses a particular realm of facts – facts that settle what you meant – and says, not that we don't *know* them, but that there *aren't* any.

In spite of this difference, *both* forms of scepticism put pressure on ordinary beliefs and practices. Cartesian scepticism threatens ordinary beliefs about the nature of the external world. How can you be justified in believing that you are not being deceived by a demon? Kripke's scepticism threatens ordinary *utterances* about meaning. How can we be justified in asserting (or denying) things like 'Jones means addition by "plus"' if there are no facts around to settle the issue?

Now a *sceptical solution* to the sceptic's argument *concedes* that the sceptic's arguments are unanswerable, and that his conclusion is correct, but *rejects* the further conclusion that the beliefs or practices threatened by it are indeed unjustified (W:66). It is to be contrasted with a *straight* solution which seeks to point out a flaw in the sceptic's initial argument that we do not know the facts in question (or that there are none). Kripke presents a sceptical solution, not a straight one (W:69).

How might a sceptical solution run? Kripke mentions two strategies: it might describe the *causes* of the threatened beliefs or practices in a way that shows them somehow to be justified. Or it might *analyse* those beliefs or practices in a way that shows them somehow to be justified (W:66–7).

Hume (according to Kripke) adopted the *first* strategy with regard to induction. His own sceptical argument seemed to show that neither logic nor experience can give you reason to expect the next emerald to be green given that all emeralds so far examined have been green. The sceptical solution *concedes* that the expectation can never be rationally justified but states that its *cause* is simply a conditioned response to our earlier exposure to uniformly green emeralds – and so the expectation in question neither has *nor needs* any *rational* justification (W: 67[1]).

Berkeley (again according to Kripke) adopted the second strategy with regard to his *metaphysical* scepticism about matter. He believed that there *is* no material substance: but does this not threaten our everyday beliefs about material objects such as tables and mountains? No, replies Berkeley: those beliefs are on a correct analysis not about *matter* at all (W:64). They are about ideas in somebody's mind. The reason I am justified in thinking e.g. that there is a desk in my study when I am not in it is because I am justified in believing what Berkeley says are alternative analyses of that utterance (*Principles* 3): that if I *were* in my study then I *would* have an idea of a desk, or that God or somebody else *is* perceiving it.

Now Kripke's sceptical solution follows the second strategy. The sceptical argument shows that there are no facts around to settle whether Jones means addition by plus: it therefore appears to threaten our justification for saying, or denying, 'Jones means addition by "plus"'. Kripke's solution is that the sceptic is right to say that there are no facts around of this sort, but he is wrong to infer that our ordinary practices of meaning ascription are unjustified, as can be seen from a proper analysis of the latter.

5.1.2 Truth-Conditions and Justification-Conditions

The allusion to Berkeley seems to illuminate by contrast a feature of Kripke's scepticism that makes it immune to sceptical solution along Berkeleian lines. Berkeley's solution was that the propriety of 'There is a desk in my study' consists in its not describing a fact about matter but rather *another* fact about what I *would* or God *does* perceive. If Kripke's solution is to parallel this approach then it seems that he must interpret 'Jones means addition by "plus"' as describing some fact whose existence even the sceptic will grant.

But how is this possible? The sceptic's whole point was that there is *no fact at all* for 'Jones means addition by "plus"' to describe. So we cannot respond to him by interpreting 'Jones means addition by "plus"' as being about some fact that the sceptic has overlooked. Any solution that uncovers such a fact would be a straight and not a sceptical solution (W:69). As Kripke puts the difficulty:

> Wittgenstein holds, with the sceptic, that there is no fact as to whether I mean plus or quus. But if this is to be conceded to the sceptic, is this not the end of the matter? What *can* be said on behalf of our ordinary attributions of meaningful language to ourselves and to others? Has not the incredible and self-defeating conclusion, that all language is meaningless, already been drawn? (W:70-1)

In reply we need to consider a crucial divergence between Kripke's sceptical solution and Berkeley's.

The general point is this. Language is a system of signs that play a certain role in human affairs. But its role need not be confined to *description*. Consider as an analogy the role of monetary instruments like coins and notes. These function e.g. as a store of wealth and a medium of exchange. Now because of certain conventions I may be *justified* in giving you a £1 coin e.g. if you are a shopkeeper who has just given me five apples at 20 pence each. But it need not follow – and in fact it is false – that either the coin itself or my act of giving it to you is a *description* of anything. It is true that certain facts must obtain if my act is justified (e.g. the fact that you can go on to exchange it for other goods and services, and maybe the existence of a central bank and gold reserves). But we can distinguish facts that need to obtain for an act to be justified from those (if any) that it describes.

Now why couldn't some declarative sentences be like money? Their utterance is justified by the role they play. But they need not be descriptions of any fact. It is just this rather liberal notion of justification that Kripke applies to meaning-ascriptions. These ascriptions have a justification that does not require *facts* about meaning. We can therefore grant with the sceptic that there are no such facts while insisting that meaning-ascriptions may be justified:

> All that is needed to legitimize assertions that someone means something is that there be roughly specifiable circumstances under which they are legitimately assertable, and that the game of asserting them under such conditions has a role in our lives. No supposition that 'facts correspond' to those assertions is needed. (W:77–8)

The sceptical solution is a specification of those circumstances and that role.

I conclude with one general point about it. As here interpreted the sceptical argument shows that there is no fact in virtue of which one associates this rather than that truth-condition with any sentence. But if it shows this much then it also shows that there is no fact in virtue of which a speaker associates this rather than that *assertibility*-condition with any sentence. Suppose I claim to associate with the sentence 'Fido has rabies' the assertibility-condition that Fido is foaming at the mouth. The sceptic will ask: in virtue of what fact have I associated *that* assertibility-condition with 'Fido has rabies' and not the condition that Fido is *quoaming* at the mouth, where to quoam means ...? A speaker's conscious association of assertibility-conditions with a sentence would *guide* his use of that sentence just as much as his association of truth-conditions with it. The factuality of such an association is therefore equally vulnerable to the sceptic who rejects the whole idea of guidance by an object of awareness. No mental image, disposition, etc., could tell me whether 'Fido has rabies' is assertible any more than it could tell me whether it was true.

If Kripke is looking amongst the *facts* for assertibility-conditions for 'Jones means addition by "plus"', doesn't it follow that this search is just as doomed as was that for its truth-conditions? Not necessarily. By 'assertibility-conditions' Kripke need *not* mean conditions that the speaker consciously associates with 'Jones means addition by "plus" ', awareness of which guides his use of it. All he means is this: conditions that as a matter of fact *bring about* in ordinary circumstances one's assertion of that sentence. Stating the assertibility-conditions of 'Jones means addition by "plus" ' is therefore not a claim about the content of 'Jones means addition by "plus" '.[2]

5.1.3 The Coherence and Scope of Scepticism

We saw that according to Kripke statements ascribing meaning to somebody need not be factual. He is therefore denying that they are *truth-conditional*: their meaning doesn't depend on any facts that settle their truth-value. Call this *non-factualism* about meaning statements.

Some commentators say that Kripke is withholding truth-conditionality not just from meaning-ascriptions but from *all* sentences:[3] as they say, Kripke is involved in *global* rather than *local* non-factualism. So according to their Kripke not only 'Jones means addition by "plus" ' but also 'The cat sat on the mat' doesn't get its meaning from 'corresponding facts' but rather from the circumstances in which it may be asserted.

The reason it matters whether Kripke is a global non-factualist is that global non-factualism can apparently be shown incoherent (Kusch 2006:154–8). Fortunately Kripke was *not* a global non-factualist (as I now argue). So I won't be exploring the arguments against global non-factualism.

What is the case for attributing global non-factualism to Kripke? It is typically based on his endorsement of Wittgenstein's later rejection of the *Tractatus* view that *all* meaningful sentences are truth-conditional. For example, Wright's case for the attribution is as follows:

[Kripke] quotes with approval (p. 73) Michael Dummett's suggestion that the central contrast between the picture of language and meaning proposed in the *Tractatus* and that of the investigations resides in a shift from a conception of statement-meaning as truth-conditional to the view that the meaning of *each* statement is fixed by its association with conditions of justified assertion. (Wright 1984:104 – my emphasis)

But when we turn to the passage of Dummett that Kripke quotes with approval we see that it runs as follows:

> The *Investigations* contains implicitly a rejection of the classical (realist) Frege-*Tractatus* view that the general form of explanation of meaning is a statement of the truth conditions. (W:73)

But this passage does *not* ascribe to the *Investigations* the view that *no* statement is truth-conditional, only a denial that they *all* are. So endorsement of it doesn't involve Kripke in global non-factualism. Similarly, Boghossian (1989:154) cites the following passage:

> If we suppose that facts or truth conditions are of the essence of meaningful assertion, it will follow from the sceptical conclusion that assertions that anyone ever means anything are meaningless. On the other hand, if we apply to these assertions the tests suggested [i.e. whether they are assertable and useful] ... no such conclusion follows. All that is needed to legitimize assertions that someone means something is that there be roughly specifiable circumstances under which they are legitimately assertable, and that the game of asserting them under such conditions has a role in our lives. No supposition that 'facts correspond' to those assertions is needed. (W:77–8)

This passage rejects the idea that facts are of the *essence* of meaningful assertion, i.e. it denies that *every* meaningful statement 'corresponds to facts'. It does *not* say that *no* meaningful statement corresponds to facts. I cannot find any passage in W where Kripke makes that claim.[4]

Other commentators have gone to the opposite pole: for them, Kripke doesn't even represent Wittgenstein as a *local* non-factualist.[5] The key passage in this connection is as follows:

> Wittgenstein's sceptical solution concedes to the sceptic that no 'truth conditions' or 'corresponding facts' in the world exist that make a statement like 'Jones, like many of us, means addition by "+"' true. Rather we should look at how such assertions are *used*. Can this be adequate? Do we not call assertions like the one just quoted 'true' or 'false'? Can we not with propriety precede

such assertions with 'It is a fact that' or 'It is not a fact that'? Wittgenstein's way with such objections is short. Like many others, Wittgenstein accepts the 'redundancy' theory of truth: to affirm that a statement is true (or, presumably, to precede it with 'It is a fact that ...') is simply to affirm the statement itself, and to say that it is not true is to deny it: ('p' is true $= p$). (W:86)

Now it seems that Kripke has contradicted himself. On the one hand he says there is no fact in virtue of which Jones means addition; on the other hand he concedes the legitimacy of 'Jones means addition by "plus"' and hence also that of 'It is a *fact* that Jones means addition by "plus"'. How can he have it both ways?[6]

According to Byrne (1996:342) we can only solve this puzzle by distinguishing what *Kripke* thinks from what he attributes to *Wittgenstein*. Byrne's analysis is as follows.

Wittgenstein holds (i) the theory of facts just quoted. But he also holds (ii) that there *are* facts about meaning. It is just that he grants (iii) that there are no *'superlative' mental* facts about meaning. Finally, he holds (iv) that when we ordinarily speak of what Jones means, etc., we are *not* saying something that implies the existence of *superlative mental* facts. So according to Wittgenstein we can say with perfect propriety and indeed truth both 'Jones means addition by "plus"' and 'It is a fact that Jones means addition by "plus"'. This explains the passage just quoted.

Now Kripke (still according to Byrne) differs from Wittgenstein in *rejecting* (iv). Hence according to *Kripke* it follows from (iii) (on which both parties agree) that (ii) is false. And although Kripke thinks that Wittgenstein rejects non-factualism, he none the less attributes it to Wittgenstein because *he* (Kripke) infers it from (iii).

> That is why Kripke (misleadingly) says that 'Wittgenstein holds, with the sceptic, that there is no fact as to whether I mean plus or quus.' More carefully, this is a thesis that Kripke believes that Wittgenstein (given the soundness of the sceptical argument) *ought* to hold. But as Kripke makes perfectly plain in the passage from p. 86 quoted above, he believes that Wittgenstein does *not* hold it. (Byrne 1996:342)

In short, the apparent contradiction is resolved once we see that it is *Kripke* who holds that there are no meaning-facts and his *Wittgenstein* who denies it.

There are two reasons for dissatisfaction with this. Firstly, according to it Kripke is being repeatedly and emphatically misleading. At a number of places he has Wittgenstein saying that there are no meaning-facts *anywhere*.[7] Not only that, but the interpretation has Kripke violating his own explicit policy of not attempting to speak for himself except 'in occasional and minor asides' (W:ix).

Secondly, the position that Kripke supposedly attributes to Wittgenstein is conservative in a quite unmotivated way. It is that there *are* facts about whether you meant addition, only not 'superlative mental' ones. It is quite unclear what 'superlative' is supposed to mean. But anyway, if the sceptical argument works at all then it cannot be contained in this way. If it works at all then it shows that there are no internal *or* external facts about meaning (as Kripke puts it: W:69). It is unclear how the argument of W Chapter 2 could possibly motivate the view that there *are* facts about meaning, only they are not mental.

A more satisfactory reading emerges from two points. (A) The word 'fact' can be understood in two ways. On one interpretation, to say that *p* states a fact is to say that it corresponds to some feature of reality. And saying that *p* is a factual statement is saying that its truth or falsity depends on whether or not some feature of reality obtains. Call this 'robust factuality'. On the second interpretation, when we say that *p* states a fact we are simply repeating *p*. And saying that *p* is fact-stating in *this* sense means only that it is *grammatically* suited to figure in such contexts as 'It is a fact that ...', i.e. it is a declarative sentence. Call this 'minimal factuality'. Thus e.g. someone who thought that ethical claims answer to no feature of reality would call 'Murder is wrong' minimally but not robustly factual.

Note that some such distinction is mandatory if we are to make any sense of W:86 at all. For the quoted passage is immediately followed by what Kripke presents as an objection to it:

However, one might object: (a) that only utterances of certain forms are called 'true' or 'false' – questions, for example, are not

– and these are so called precisely because they purport to state facts.

Now if 'fact' here means the same as the 'fact' of which Wittgenstein asserts a redundancy theory, then how can this passage possibly constitute an *objection* to that theory? It sounds like a *restatement* of it. The difficulty vanishes, however, if we understand 'fact' here in the robust sense.

(B) We need to distinguish two persons: the *actual* Wittgenstein and the person that Kripke chooses to *represent* Wittgenstein as being. Call these two characters W1 and W2. Kripke himself warns that they are distinct (W:5, 70–1) and it is here that the distinction is relevant.

Then my reading of the quoted passage from W:86 is as follows. In the first sentence Kripke attributes to W2 the view that statements about meaning are not *robustly* factual. Then he states the objection. Then he states W1's reply: that the only notion of factuality he recognizes is the minimal one. Hence for W1, the thesis that there are no facts about meaning, if it can be stated at all, says something false. This is of course consistent with the view earlier attributed to W1 that:

> Whenever our opponent insists on the perfect propriety of an ordinary form of expression [e.g. that it is a *fact* that you meant addition by plus] ..., we can insist that if these expressions are properly understood, we agree. The danger comes when we try to give a precise formulation of exactly what it is that we *are* denying – *what* 'erroneous interpretation' our opponent is placing on ordinary means of expression. (W:70)

W2 on the contrary is someone who risks that danger. For him, both the robust *and* the minimal conception of fact are available: and his point is that meaning-ascriptions are minimally but not *robustly* factual. Thus for W2, if 'fact' is understood in the minimal way then 'It is a fact that Jones meant addition by plus' is no worse off than 'Jones means addition by "plus"'. But if 'fact' is understood in the robust sense – which he differs from W1 in finding legitimate – then 'It is a fact that Jones means addition by "plus"' is indeed a precise formulation of what W2 is claiming to deny.

In short: there was a tension between W:86 and Kripke's

attribution of non-factualism to Wittgenstein. It is best resolved by distinguishing – not Kripke from his Wittgenstein but – W1 from W2. W:86, like W:70–1, is one of those points where Kripke briefly discusses W1 before resuming exegesis of W2, who is the main character of the drama. This interpretation has the advantage of not making Kripke's attributions of non-factualism to Wittgenstein misleading expressions of his own view: he is rather attributing them to W2, and not himself or W1. Its price is that we must impute to Kripke two distinctions: that between W1 and W2 and that between robust and minimal factuality.[8] But Kripke himself makes the first explicit; and the second is as we have seen required by the *internal* coherence of W:86, regardless of its relation to the rest of the text.

So it seems to me that neither the 'global non-factualist' nor the 'factualist' interpretation is textually plausible. Kripke represents Wittgenstein as a *local* non-factualist about *meaning*-statements *only*.[9]

As we saw, he also thinks that despite their not expressing facts we are still justified in using them: that is the sceptical solution. And he grounds this justification in their assertibility-conditions and utility. Let us now consider Kripke's account of these.

5.2 DETAIL OF THE SCEPTICAL SOLUTION

At W: 86–95 Kripke states the assertibility-conditions and utility of meaning ascriptions. At 5.2.1 I discuss the assertibility-conditions for 'one person considered in isolation'. (W:87–8; 90–1). At 5.2.2 I discuss the assertibility-conditions for those ascriptions in a com-munitarian context (W:88–91). At 5.2.3 I discuss the utility that Kripke attributes to those statements (W:92–5). These three con-ditions form the premises of the argument against private language discussed at 5.3.

5.2.1 'One Person Considered in Isolation'
Kripke introduces the case of one person considered in isolation with the remark that the sceptical paradox

> holds no terrors in our daily lives; no one actually hesitates when asked to produce an answer to an addition problem! Almost all of us unhesitatingly answer '125' when asked for the sum of 68

and 57, without any thought to the theoretical possibility that a quus-like rule might have been appropriate! And we do so without justification. (W:87)

Now it isn't quite true that we answer *addition* problems without justification: if asked for a justification we might describe a certain method for reaching that conclusion. We might say that we added 8 and 7, then put down the 5 and carried the 1, etc. What is true is that when we answer an addition problem we proceed by carrying out certain steps that cannot *themselves* be justified. For instance we carry the 1 rather than *quarrying* the 1 (where to 'quarry' the 1 means to carry it if both summands are less than 57, otherwise to write down '5' and leave that as the answer). And we do *this* without justification.

It is important to realize that from now on Kripke's argument will focus on these basic steps out of which any procedure by which we answer an addition (or any other) problem is composed. It is these basic steps – these applications of rules that are not themselves justified in terms of other rules – of which it can truly be said that we carry them out both unhesitatingly and without justification. Now if an individual who is in some sense 'private' cannot be said to mean anything by the descriptions that he gives of these basic steps (e.g. he cannot be said to mean carry rather than quarry by 'carry'), then neither can he mean anything by the descriptions that he gives of the upshots of procedures that involve them (e.g. addition rather than quaddition by 'plus'). It therefore suffices to focus attention on cases where the subject's application of expressions is in this sense basic.

'Plus' will not serve this purpose. Our applications of 'plus' *can* be justified by appeal to other rules (although those justifications themselves perhaps cannot). So from now on I consider another case: application of the predicate 'red' to some object visible in normal light. It is plausible that a subject's application of 'red' in cases like these is both unhesitating and unjustified: so if Kripke's account applies anywhere it applies here. So the question we need to address is this: what are the assertibility-conditions, for one person considered in isolation, of meaning-ascriptions involving 'red'?

Kripke continues:

It is part of our language game of speaking of rules that a person

147

may, without ultimately giving any justification, follow his own confident inclination (say, [calling this object 'red']) is the *right* way to respond, rather than another way [e.g. calling it 'yellow']. That is, the 'assertability conditions' that license an individual to say that, on a given occasion, he ought to follow the rule this way rather than that, are, ultimately, that he does what he is inclined to do. (W:87–8)

(I have replaced Kripke's arithmetical example with my chromatic one for the reason just given. Thus for the remainder of the discussion.)

Kripke is saying this: it is a feature of our language that a speaker is entitled to say that calling something 'red' is the *right* response just in case he *is* in fact inclined to call it 'red'. Hence a speaker who applies the word 'red' to something is also entitled to say that that application is correct. Saying that his present application of 'red' is correct does not amount simply to a repetition of the claim that the object is in fact red. It is the further claim that this use of 'red' is the way he ought to follow the rule for 'red'. Or equivalently: that calling it 'red' accords with what he meant all along. So we could put the claim slightly more clearly as follows. Suppose that a speaker is confronted with a particular object in normal light. And consider the claim:

(1) The application of 'red' to this object accords with what I meant by 'red' all along (i.e. up until now)

Then the claim is that (1) is assertible for the speaker just in case he is inclined to apply 'red' to the object.

We can derive from this claim a corresponding assertibility-condition for a first-personal meaning-ascription. Consider the statement:

(2) By 'red' I meant all along a predicate that applies to this object

A person is entitled to assert (2) just in case he is prepared sincerely to apply the predicate 'red' to this object.

Now what is important is that one's preparedness to apply 'red' to this object is the one and only thing that is relevant to the assertibility of (1) and (2). What else could be relevant? Suppose I cast my mind back over my training in the use of 'red', my previous uses of that word, and indeed *others'* uses of that word. The whole point of the sceptical argument is that *nothing* in these objects of awareness *tells* me whether or not to apply 'red' to *this* object. For those facts about the past are compatible with *any* future application of that word (W:88). The only thing that settles whether or not to assert (1) and (2) is my present brute inclination to *apply* 'red' to this object.

It seems to me that if we confine attention to *my* grounds for asserting (1) then this must be the correct account of the matter. At any rate the account is correct if we assume (as I do throughout this chapter) that the sceptical arguments themselves are sound.

The situation is comparable to that entailed by a natural account of *doxastic* self-ascription. When am I entitled to assert that I believe that *p*? I am entitled to assert it just in case I am inclined sincerely to assert *p* itself. It is not as though I look within myself to see if I can find the belief hanging around in my mind. What I do is ask myself whether *p* itself is true. And if I am inclined to say that it *is* then I am entitled to assert that I *believe* that it is. Similarly, no amount of looking inside myself, or at my training or past usage, will settle whether or not I assert (1) and (2). What matters is whether I am inclined to call this object 'red': the presence or absence of that inclination is necessary and sufficient to settle my entitlement to assert (1) and (2).

It is perhaps worth noting an assumption that has been implicit throughout this discussion: that by assertibility-conditions of meaning-ascriptions for 'one person considered in isolation' Kripke means the assertibility-conditions of *first-personal* meaning-ascriptions. It is clear that Kripke *is* concerned with first-personal meaning-ascriptions. He says that a speaker 'may... follow *his* own confident inclination that this way... is the right way to respond' (W:87 – my emphasis). He says that when we consider a 'private' language user (by which he means an individual considered in isolation – W:109–10) we are concerned with '*his* justification-conditions alone' (W:89). He implicitly contrasts the assertibility-conditions for one person considered in isolation with those for *others* in his community (W:89). And his clearest statement of the assertibility-conditions of meaning-statements *explicitly* contrasts first- and third- personal assertibility-conditions (W:90–1 – see 5.2.2 for discussion). It therefore seems clear to me that the first part of the sceptical solution, the part directed at assertibility-conditions of meaning-ascriptions for 'one person considered in isolation', is a claim about first-personal meaning ascriptions like (1) and (2).

To summarize that claim: the assertibility-conditions for first-personal ascriptions of meaning like (1) or (2) are settled by my present brute inclination to apply the word whose meaning they concern. And this is the first part of the sceptical solution.

5.2.2 Meaning-Ascriptions in a Social Context

The second part concerns assertibility-conditions for meaning-ascriptions in the *third* person. When are we licensed to say of another e.g. that his present application of 'red' conforms to what he meant by it all along? When are we licensed to say of him that by 'red' he meant a predicate that applies to this object rather than one that does not?

Kripke starts by discussing the case of a teacher and a pupil. Replacing his arithmetical example with my chromatic one, the gist of his discussion (W:89–90) is that a teacher is entitled to say that a student has grasped the teacher's meaning of 'red' (or as the teacher would say, that he means red by 'red') only if the pupil's applications of 'red' *agree* with the teacher's (or with the applications that the teacher is sincerely inclined to make). At any rate this must be true for straightforward cases, e.g. chromatically uniform objects that are viewed close-up in normal light. If the pupil but not the teacher applies 'red' to a distantly glimpsed object, or one viewed in poor or changing light, then the teacher may still say that the student means red by 'red'. But if only one of them applies 'red' to a rose viewed from six inches in bright sunlight then the teacher is not entitled to maintain that judgement.

Kripke then considers the case where one ascribes meaning to another adult – or rather where one says that another adult is applying an expression in accordance with what he meant all along (W:90). He says that A is entitled to say that B is no longer applying an expression in accordance with what B meant all along *if* the following two things are true: (i) B's application of the expression up until now accords with A's application of it (or the applications that he was sincerely inclined to make); (ii) B's *current* application of the expression does *not* accord with A's application of it (or the application that A is sincerely inclined to make) – at any rate so long as the application in question is basic in the sense of 5.2.1 (e.g.

the application of 'red' to some object viewed from close-up in normal light).

From these two points we can extract the following assertibility-conditions for third-personal meaning ascriptions. From the discussion of the teacher/pupil case we can say something about the assertibility of the following statement:

(3) Jones means red by 'red'

What we can say is that a *necessary* condition for (3) to be assertible by Smith is that Jones's applications of the predicate 'red' agree with *Smith's* applications of that predicate. And from the discussion of the 'adult' case we can say something about the assertibility of the following statement:

(4) Jones's present application of 'red' does *not* accord with what he meant all along

What we can say is that a *sufficient* condition for (4) to be assertible by Smith is that Jones's application of 'red' has hitherto agreed with Smith's but his *present* application of 'red' does *not* agree with Smith's inclination to apply or withhold 'red'. These two points (the assertibility-conditions of (3) and (4)) together form the second part of the sceptical solution.

It may be objected that the assertibility-condition for (3) is false on the grounds that *agreement* between Smith's applications and Jones's is not a necessary condition for Smith's finding (3) assertible. One might say this on the grounds that the following proposal (adapted from Goldfarb 1985: 102) correctly specifies a *sufficient* condition on Smith's finding (3) assertible:

(5) It is licensed to assert that Jones means red by 'red' when he has applied 'red' to all and only *red* things about whose colour he has been queried

Now (5) does not say anything about agreement between Smith's responses and Jones's. Since (5) plausibly does give sufficient conditions for the assertibility of (3) it appears that agreement between Smith's responses and Jones's cannot be necessary for the assertibility of (3) itself.

However this appearance is an illusion because (5) is false.

Suppose that Jones *does* apply 'red' to all and only the red things on whose colour Smith has tested him; but suppose also that Smith is *not* inclined to call all those things 'red'. Then it seems plain that Smith will *not* be in a position to assert (3). So (5) is false (or it is sufficient after all for agreement between Smith and Jones). Of course it is true that Smith would *assent* to the sentence labelled (5). But this is nothing to the point; it is still true that (5) does not give a correct sufficient condition for Smith's finding (3) assertible.

There are indeed some cases where widespread agreement is *not* a necessary condition for asserting a sentence of the form of (3). Suppose that Smith thinks himself to be very bad at adding anything but the smallest numbers but regards Jones as having a very high level of mathematical aptitude. Then it is likely that Smith will find 'Jones means addition by "+"' to be assertible as long as Jones gives confident answers to a variety of addition problems; there need be no additional prerequisite that Jones's answers in *complex* cases agree with Smith's. The reason that widespread agreement is violated in this case is of course that we are considering applications of '+' that are not basic. It remains true that Smith will assert 'Jones means addition by "+"' only if he – Smith – thinks that Jones's answers in the *simplest* cases agree with those that Smith is inclined to give (see the long parenthetical remark at W:91).

So far we have seen the first two parts of the sceptical solution: one part concerns first-personal assertibility-conditions and the other part concerns third-personal assertibility-conditions. Kripke summarizes both parts of the sceptical solution as follows:

> *Jones* is entitled... provisionally and subject to correction by others, to judge a new response to be 'correct' simply because it is the response he is inclined to give... But Smith need *not* accept Jones's authority on these matters: *Smith* will judge Jones to mean [red by 'red'] only if he judges that Jones's answers to particular [colour-identification] problems agree with those *he* is inclined to give, or, if they occasionally disagree, he can interpret Jones as at least following the proper procedure... If Jones consistently fails to give responses in agreement... with Smith's, Smith will judge that he does not mean [red by 'red']. Even if Jones did mean it in the past, the present deviation will justify Smith in judging that he has lapsed. (W:90–1)

Before moving on to the third part of the sceptical solution it is worth briefly addressing one puzzling element in this passage. When describing the first-personal (i.e. Jones's) assertibility-conditions Kripke states that they are 'provisional and subject to correction by others'. This remark appears to subvert the whole drift of 5.2.1. For it was argued there that *nothing* other than Jones's inclination to apply 'red' in the present instance is relevant to his finding assertible the claims there labelled (1) and (2). And this must include the responses of others, including their 'corrections'. But now it appears that Kripke has significantly weakened that claim.

In fact he has not – at least that reading of the passage is not mandatory. To say that Jones's self-ascriptions of (1) and (2) are 'subject to correction by others' need *not* mean that Smith's opinion is relevant to the assertibility of (1) and (2) for Jones. An alternative – and in the context more charitable – reading is this: Smith is entitled to *reject* Jones's self-ascriptions *notwithstanding* (and so compatibly with) Jones's continuing entitlement to *assert* it. So Kripke does not mean that Jones's entitlement to assert (1) and (2) depends on Smith's not being prepared to endorse (4). It is rather that *Smith's* entitlement to reject (4) is *not* affected by Jones's being in a position to endorse (1) and (2). On this reading the remark that Jones 'is subject to correction' *is* compatible with the view that nothing other than Jones's present inclinations are relevant to *his* entitlement to (1) and (2). So that is probably what Kripke meant.

5.2.3 *The Utility of Meaning-Ascriptions*

As well as requiring a statement of the assertibility-conditions for meaning-ascriptions Kripke thinks that their rehabilitation entails an account of their *utility*.

What then is the use of saying things like 'Jones means red by "red"'? According to Kripke its use is that it licenses predictions concerning Jones's behaviour (W:92–3). More precisely, it supports the expectation that Jones's applications of the word 'red' in future will agree with everyone else's. This is obviously of practical importance. I will only ask Jones to go to the grocer's to get me 'five red apples' if I expect him to apply the word 'red' in the same way as I do. Otherwise he could for all I know return with five *green* apples (or at any rate five apples that *I'd* call 'green').

It is true that there is more to the utility of meaning-ascriptions than the evident fact just stated, at least when it comes to ascribing to Jones a grasp of terms whose application is more complex. Thus suppose that Smith knows that Jones has greater mathematical ability than Smith. Then the utility for Smith of the assertion that Jones means addition by '+' need not lie only in the fact that Jones's response will agree with Smith's in simple cases. It has the following additional utility: Smith will expect Jones (though he may not expect himself) to respond to relatively *complex* queries of the form '$x + y$?' with the *sum* of x and y. So Jones will be able to use Smith as a kind of arithmetical prosthesis. And *this* utility goes beyond that of future agreement in simple cases. However the possible presence of this additional utility does not (as we shall see) affect the relevance of Kripke's utility claim for his argument against private language.

Nor does it affect the following remark. Our initial conception of meaning took INR as axiomatic: Jones's meaning red by 'red' was supposed to be a mental state of him that somehow *guided* his behaviour (see 4.1.3). So we seemed to be postulating a mysterious *nexus* between what Jones means and what he does: if Jones means red by 'red', and intends to give the right answer to chromatic queries, then he *must* call visibly red items 'red' (cf. W:65). But we learnt from the sceptical argument that INR cannot be satisfied: there is neither guidance nor compulsion here. But now we see the true meaning of the 'nexus' idea: only the nexus is not in Jones but in *us*. It isn't some mysterious state of Jones that somehow tells him what to do: it is rather that if *we* judge that he means red by 'red' then *we* will expect him to apply 'red' in the same way as us. And if he does not then we will conclude that in fact he did not mean red by 'red'. The inexorability of the rule that Jones grasps for 'red' is not some super-rigid mechanism in *Jones's* mind: it is rather a rigidly applied expectation, concerning Jones's behaviour, in Smith's:

We say: 'If you really follow the rule in multiplying, you *must* all get the same result.' Now if this is only the somewhat hysterical way of putting things that you get in university talk, it need not interest us overmuch. It is however the expression of an attitude towards the technique of calculation, which comes out everywhere in our life. The emphasis of the *must* corresponds only to the inexorableness of this attitude, both to the technique of calculating and to a host of related techniques. (Wittgenstein 1978: 430 (VII-67))

5.2.4 Conclusion

Kripke's sceptical solution covers three points: the assertibility of meaning-ascriptions in the first- and third-personal case, and their utility. I argued that Kripke's discussion of their utility does not exhaust it. But this is irrelevant to what follows. Those parts of Kripke's claims that *are* relevant as follows:

(i) Jones is entitled to assert: 'By "red" I meant all along a predicate that applies to this object' if and only if he is inclined to apply 'red' to this object

(ii) Smith is entitled to assert: 'Jones's present application of "red" does *not* accord with what he meant all along' if Jones's inclinations to apply 'red' have so far agreed with Smith's but his *present* one does not

(iii) Smith is entitled to assert: 'Jones means red by "red"' only if Jones's inclinations to apply 'red' have so far agreed with Smith's

(iv) The utility of a meaning-ascription is that it licenses Smith's expectation that Jones's *future* applications of red will agree with Smith's

These four points will in certain combinations form the premises of three arguments, all in a sense against 'private language'. At any rate that is what I will now argue.

5.3 THE ARGUMENT AGAINST PRIVATE LANGUAGE

I begin by asking what the conclusion of the argument against private language is supposed to be. I suggest two possibilities before describing and assessing the arguments for each.

5.3.1 What is its Conclusion?

There are various things that Kripke's (and Wittgenstein's) private language argument have been thought to establish:

(A) An individual who does not communicate with others cannot mean anything by his words

(B) An individual cannot use words to refer to items that only he has *knowledge* of

(C) An individual cannot use words that only he can *understand*

(D) An individual cannot use words to refer to items that only he can *possess*

(E) An individual cannot use words to refer to items (e.g. phenomenal states) that have no correlation with publicly available items (e.g. behaviour)

(F) An individual cannot fix the reference of words denoting phenomenal states without reference to correlated public criteria
(G) Meaning-ascriptions cannot be governed solely by the assertibility-conditions available to an individual considered in isolation
(H) We cannot ascribe meaning to anyone unless there is sufficient agreement in our community

There is some interrelation between these claims. (B) follows from (C) given the contestable assumption that one can only understand terms that refer to items of which he can have knowledge. (D) follows from (B) given the contestable assumption that one cannot have knowledge of states that one cannot possess. (E) follows from (F) given the contestable assumption that you cannot use a word to refer to something unless you can fix the reference of a word denoting that thing. (E) follows from (B) given the contestable assumption that one cannot have knowledge of states of another that have no publicly available correlate (as e.g. pain-behaviour is such a correlate of pain). (E) follows from (I) given the contestable assumption that if you use a term to refer to something that has no publicly available correlate then I cannot tell whether your use of it agrees with mine (W:99–100; 100n81).

Which of these is Kripke aiming at?

Certainly (A) is the most spectacular. We might call it the 'Robinson Crusoe' hypothesis. For it seems to imply that Robinson Crusoe could not have kept a diary when he was alone on the island. Whether or not (A) does imply this depends on whether it is a claim about one person when he is incommunicado or only as a claim about the *congenitally* uncommunicative. In the latter case it implies nothing about Robinson Crusoe, who did communicate with others in his early life. Be that as it may Kripke is quite clear that he does not endorse (A) on any reading (W:110); so indeed was Wittgenstein (1967 section 243).

Now Wittgenstein himself certainly had an interest in (B) and (C); and he seems to have held that (B) follows from (C) (1967: section 243). He also indicates a specific interest in (D) (section 253), (E) (section 270) and (F) (section 258). But *Kripke's* private language argument is never presented as an argument for any of (B)-(F), which I have mentioned only so as to fix in the reader's mind their distinctness from the former, and also to distinguish Kripke's concerns from (the real) Wittgenstein's. He does mention (C) but only because he thinks that it follows from his official conclusion (W:109–110). He also mentions (E) but again only in the context of a more general claim that he has already defended (W:99–100).

I think that Kripke's text does provide the materials of a case for both (G) and (H). As we shall see, (G) is probably the 'official' message of Kripke's private language argument. But it and (H) are both interesting and both discernible in the text. So I will simply examine the case for each.

5.2.2 The Case for (G)

Claim (G) is that meaning-ascriptions cannot be made on the basis of the assertibility-conditions available to an individual considered in isolation. On my interpretation this means that there cannot be an institution of meaning-ascription governed solely by its first-personal assertibility-conditions. What *this* claim amounts to, and what further consequences it has, will become clearer if we consider the argument for it.

That argument appears straight after Kripke has argued for the assertibility-conditions of first-personal meaning-ascriptions i.e. the claims labelled (i) and (ii) at 5.2.4. Kripke writes:

> Someone... may, under the influence of a drug, suddenly act in accordance with a quus-like rule changing from his first intentions. If there could be no justification for saying... that he is no longer in accord with the rule that he previously followed, there would be little content to our idea that a rule, or past intention, *binds* future choices. We are inclined to accept conditionals of such a rough type as, 'If someone means [red by "red"] then, if he remembers his past intention and wishes to conform to it, when he is queried about [the colour of a visibly red object], he will answer ["red"].' The question is what substantive content such conditionals have. If our considerations so far are correct, the answer is that, if one person is considered in isolation, the notion of a rule as guiding the person who adopts it can have *no* substantive content. (W:88–9)

The argument in this passage may be stated as follows:

(1) Meaning-ascriptions only count as such if the following condition holds: there are possible conditions under which it is licensed to say

that Jones's *present* application of 'red' is *not* in accordance with what he meant by it up until now (premise)

(2) If meaning-ascriptions are governed solely by the assertibility-conditions for one person considered in isolation then they do not conform to this condition (premise)

(3) Therefore meaning-ascriptions are *not* governed solely by the assertibility-conditions for an individual in isolation (from 3)

The step from (1) and (2) to (3) appears to be valid. So there are two remaining questions. Is premise (1) true? And is premise (2) true?

Suppose that premise (1) is false. Then *no* sincere application of a word could count as a violation of one's previous meaning. But in that case there would be no distinction between using an expression in accordance with what one meant and using it however one liked. For one could never be in a position to say, of any sincere application of an expression, that it was *not* in accordance with one's prior meaning. And it seems to be essential to the concept of applying a word in accordance with what one meant that such a distinction *can* be drawn (as for instance in Kripke's illustration of the man influenced by a drug). So premise (1) appears to be true.

Premise (2) follows from part (i) of the sceptical conclusion:

(i) Jones is entitled to assert: 'By "red" I meant all along a predicate that applies to this object' if and only if he is inclined to apply 'red' to this object

It follows that if we consider only the grounds for meaning-ascriptions that are available to a person considered in isolation, there can never be grounds for *Jones* to say 'Jones is not applying red in accordance with what he meant by it'. For when could this be assertible? If Jones sincerely applies red to *any* object, he will by (i) be entitled to say that he *is* acting in accordance with what he meant all along. So it will *never* be possible for Jones to say that his present use is not in accordance with what he meant up until now.

Nor will it be possible for *us* to say that Jones is no longer acting in accordance with what he meant *if* our third-personal ascriptions of 'acting in accordance with what he meant' to Jones are parasitic upon those that govern Jones's *first*-personal ascriptions. Here 'parasitic' means this: we are not entitled to withhold the claim that Jones is acting in accordance with what he meant if Jones himself is inclined to assert that he *is*. This sort of parasitism of third- upon first-personal grounds is approximated–though not fully realized – in the case of pain-ascriptions. One's initial inclination not to judge that Jones is in pain is overruled, or at any rate weakened, by Jones's sincere inclination to assert that he *is*. Now we know from (i) that *whatever* Jones sincerely says, he will be inclined to say that he is acting in accordance with what he meant. Hence if an analogous and extreme parasitism applied to the claim that Jones's present use is faithful to what he meant all along, it would not be possible for *us* to assert that Jones has changed his meaning.

Now the antecedent of (2) – that meaning-ascriptions are governed solely by the assertibility-conditions for an individual in isolation – is to be understood as the following disjunction: *either* (a) all meaning-ascriptions are first-personal; *or* (b) all third-personal meaning-ascriptions are parasitical upon first-personal ones. The argument of the last but one paragraph established on the basis of (i) that if disjunct (a) is true then so is the consequent of (2). The argument of the last paragraph established on the basis of (i) that if disjunct (b) is true then so is the consequent of (2). Hence the argument of both paragraphs together suffices to establish (2) on the basis of part (i) of the sceptical solution. And that completes the case for (G).

It is worth pausing to say a little about the importance of (G). Claim (G) does *not* imply that Robinson Crusoe (or a congenital isolate) cannot be the subject of meaning-ascriptions. For it is perfectly compatible with (G) that *we* should ascribe meanings to Robinson Crusoe. (It is however true that if Robinson Crusoe's transitive verb 'to mean' only takes the first person then *he* cannot use it to make meaning-ascriptions.)

What (G) *does* require is that if we do so then our grounds for saying that he accords or does not accord with what he meant must be *independent* (in the sense of not being parasitic upon) *his* grounds for doing so. We must apply *our* grounds for making such claims rather than *his*. (I think this is what Kripke means by saying that we must 'take him into our community': see W:110). So Kripke is right not to endorse (A). For all that (G) says, belonging to a community is not a necessary condition on being a subject of meaning-ascriptions.

However it *is* a consequence of (G) that belonging to a community is not sufficient either. Consider a community where third-personal claims as to whether somebody accords with his previous meaning are *parasitic* upon first-personal claims in the sense previously specified. In that community nobody is ascribing meaning to anybody else: for the distinction between *seeming* to accord with what you meant and *actually* according with it is invisible to them. There must be independent third-personal grounds for making or withholding the attribution of meaning: independent, that is, of first-personal ones.

However, if a community conforms to part (ii) of the sceptical solution then it *does* meet the condition laid down in premise (1). Part (ii) says this: Smith can say that Jones does *not* accord with his previous meaning if Smith's past application of 'red' does, but his present application does not, agree with Jones's. This means that there *are* possible sincere applications of 'red' on Jones's part that Smith is entitled to regard as involving infidelity to Jones's prior intentions (cf. W:93). At least, this is so if the members of that community possess independent wills, so that their applications of an expression in a given situation might possibly diverge (cf. W:112n88). So part (ii) of the sceptical solution, though it is not strictly a premise of the private language argument, generates a kind of foil to the private linguist's predicament. It implies that that predicament is not inevitable. The obstacle that prevents Jones in isolation from ascribing meanings is a special problem for individuals considered in isolation. It will be overcome in a community that conforms to (ii).

That concludes my assessment of the importance of (G). For the reasons stated I think that Kripke's argument for it is sound.

5.3.3 The case for (H)

The point of (G) was this: it showed that meaning-ascriptions can only exist if their third-person ascription conditions are in a sense independent of their first-person ones. And we have just seen from part (ii) of the sceptical solution that this condition is met if *my* inclination to apply an expression in some given case could in principle disagree with *yours*. But Kripke also argues for another constraint on meaning-ascriptions from what you might call the opposite direction. Whilst meaning-ascriptions could not exist without the *possibility* of disagreement, they would be pointless in the presence of *widespread* disagreement:

The entire 'game' that we have described – that the community

attributes concepts to an individual so long as he exhibits sufficient conformity, under test circumstances, to the behaviour of
the community – would lose its point outside a community that
generally agrees in its practices. If one person, asked to [state the
colour of an object] answered ['red'], another ['green'], another
['yellow'], if there was no general agreement in the community
responses, the game of attributing concepts to individuals – as we
have described it – could not exist. (W:95–6)

If we interpret 'so long as' in this passage to mean 'only if' then we
have a fairly clear argument from part (iii) of the sceptical solution:
that Smith is entitled to say that Jones means red by 'red' (i.e. is
entitled to attribute a grasp of the concept) only if Smith's and
Jones's past applications of 'red' have been in agreement. The argument simply contraposes this premise and generalizes it: if nobody ever agreed on the application of any expression then nobody
would ever be entitled to say of anyone *else* that he had grasped it.
It seems clear therefore that if (iii) is true then a certain minimal
level of agreement is a necessary condition on meaning-attribution.

But if we interpret 'so long as' (perhaps more naturally) to mean
'if' then the argument appears to proceed from the equally plausible
converse of premise (iii): that Smith is entitled to say that Jones
means red by 'red' if Jones's and Smith's responses are in agreement. But it seems unclear why the converse of (iii), even if true,
should be relevant. How can the fact that interpersonal agreement
is *sufficient* for meaning-attribution be relevant to establishing that
interpersonal agreement is *necessary* for it?

The demand for agreement emerges from the converse of
(iii) – call it (iii*) – in the presence of an additional premise, part (iv)
of the sceptical solution. This claim – a claim about the *utility* of
meaning-ascriptions – said that Smith is entitled to infer, from the
statement that Jones means red by 'red', that Smith's and Jones's
applications of 'red' will agree in future. So between them, (iii*)
and (iv) specify respectively the grounds for making meaning-
ascriptions and the conclusions that can be drawn from the latter.

Now imagine a world where these conditions come apart. Suppose in particular that the following happened: people who tended
to agree on their *initial* applications of 'red' tended to *disagree* on
later applications of it. Let us call a community in which this
phenomenon occurs a *systematically divergent* community. Any two

people in it will appear to one another just as Wittgenstein's recalcitrant pupil appears to his teacher (1967: section 185). In that situation no attribution of grasp of 'red' that was licensed by (iii*) could have the utility specified by (iv). The existence in Smith's language of an expression like 'Jones means "red" by red', if governed by (iii) and (iv), would be systematically misleading. It would lead him to pass from truths to falsehoods.

For instance: Jones will initially answer 'red' when confronted with post-boxes, fire-engines and tomatoes. Smith, observing this, will by (iii*) conclude that Jones means red by 'red'. And then by (iv) he will draw the further conclusion that Jones will in future use the word 'red' in the same way that he, Smith, does. But by the assumption of systematic divergence, this expectation will be disappointed. The next time Smith asks Jones to go to the grocers to get five red apples, Jones will come back with five *green* apples – or at any rate five apples that *Smith* would call 'green'.

Therefore if (iv) correctly describes *an* essential aspect of the utility of meaning-ascriptions (it need not exhaust their utility), there could be no meaning-ascriptions in a systematically divergent community. In that community the concept of meaning ought to be rejected on the grounds that its use would lead us from true beliefs about a subject's past behaviour to false beliefs about his future behaviour. (Cf. Dummett's grounds for rejecting Bosche: 1981a:454.)

Thus it seems that the sceptical solution requires two kinds of agreement as necessary conditions on a practice of meaning-ascription. It is a consequence of part (iii) alone of the sceptical conclusion that there could be no third-personal meaning-ascriptions if there was *no* agreement amongst language-users as to the application of a predicate (or at least its basic applications in the sense of 5.2.1). And it is a consequence of (iii*) and part (iv) of the sceptical conclusion that there could be no third-personal meaning ascriptions in a community that was systematically divergent.

So if *both* parts (iii) and (iv) of the sceptical solution *and* the converse (iii*) of its part (iii) are true, then (H) itself is true on *two* interpretations of the expression 'sufficient agreement' contained within it. It is true if 'sufficient agreement' means *absence of ubiquitous disagreement*. And it is true if 'sufficient agreement' means *absence of systematic divergence*.

5.4 SUMMARY

Kripke has argued that we can give a sceptical solution to the sceptical paradox. The sceptical solution is sceptical: it involves the concession that sentences ascribing meaning (but only those) are not descriptions of any possible facts (5.1). The sceptical solution is a solution: it rehabilitates the meaningfulness of those sentences by describing conditions under which they can be asserted and the utility that such assertions have (5.2). The sceptical solution yields the following conclusions about 'private language'. First that meaning-ascriptions only count as such if their third-person assertibility conditions are independent of those that are available to one person considered in isolation (5.3.2). Second that third-person meaning-ascriptions can only be made in a community where there is neither ubiquitous nor systematic divergence in the application of linguistic expressions (5.3.3).

6

CONCLUSION

In conclusion I should like to summarize the positions defended in this book and to offer guidance to the reader who wishes to learn more about Kripke.

We saw at Chapter 2 that Kripke has not refuted the description theory of names: at any rate he has not refuted FRTC. The defender of FRTC can meet all three arguments; and in any case more needs to be said to relieve the pressure towards FRTC as outlined at 2.1.3. So what I described in the Introduction as the Lockean picture of meaning – on which it is somehow mediated by, or dependent upon, a speaker's association of a name with something like its sense – remains attractive.

We saw at Chapter 3 that Kripke has not convincingly rehabilitated metaphysics as an autonomous and substantive discipline. The arguments considered there for saying e.g. that a person has his ancestors essentially involve a heavy and in my view unacceptable reliance on 'intuition'. And even if we waive these concerns about intuition we have seen other reasons to doubt the quasi-Cartesian arguments against materialism. So even if there is a genuine science of metaphysics based upon intuition, it is unlikely to deliver as a theorem the falsity of mind-brain identity theses.

We saw at Chapter 4 that Kripke has given powerful arguments against the idea that our ordinary notion of meaning can meet the demands we place upon it: that it is something awareness of which guides your use and yet can be decisively manifested through competent performance. That these desiderata pull in opposite directions is hardly grounds for criticizing the sceptic's argument: for they were present in our intuitive conception of meaning all along.

We saw at Chapter 5 that Kripke's version of the private language argument appears to deliver three conclusions: that there is no sense to the idea that somebody can mean anything when considered in isolation; and that meaning-ascriptions have no function in communities that are either ubiquitously or systematically divergent. These conclusions do apparently follow from the sceptical solution. Whether the sceptical solution *is* the only possible response to the sceptic is another question.

There is an enormous literature that builds upon all of these Kripkean ideas. Probably the most sophisticated and extensive recent discussion of the material in NN is Soames 2002. The argument against materialism has been endlessly criticized and refined since its publication. The most notable recent version is Chalmers 1996: for a discussion of this work that the present author found especially helpful and persuasive, see Loar 1999.

Probably the most important thesis of NN not discussed in the present volume is Kripke's outline of a direct theory of reference in terms of a causal chain stretching back from the use of a name to an initial act of christening. For a vivid outline of the theory and a powerful criticism of Kripke's version of it, see Evans 1973. Recanati 1997 is a thorough and accessible discussion of the theory of direct reference.

An extremely helpful collection of articles relating to interpretative and substantial issues arising from W is Miller and Wright 2002 (extensively cited in the present book). But the most thorough discussion of W is also the most recent: Kusch 2006.

One element of W not touched upon here is the postscript on Wittgenstein on other minds. This has in fact attracted relatively little commentary. A discussion that helpfully exhibits its continuity with the main text of W is Tait 1986. Another matter that I have not discussed at all is the question of Kripke's fidelity to Wittgenstein. Kripke is extensively criticized for departing from Wittgenstein's views in Baker and Hacker 1984; for a reply, see the concluding chapter of Kusch 2006.

It will be evident from all of this that Kripke's work has had an enormous impact on the central questions of metaphysics and the philosophy of language. It will also be evident from a glance at the secondary literature that this is at odds with what I think its influence *ought* to be: the lessons of NN have in my view been swallowed too quickly, and those of W unfairly criticized. And it may be that in years to come philosophers will draw from Kripke's work conclusions that differ from those that are widely received today. Probably the only thing one can say with confidence about his ultimate influence is what Chou En-lai said about that of the French Revolution: it is too soon to tell.

ENDNOTES

2 Names

1. See e.g. Hughes 2004:15–18.
2. For this proposal to work we might also need Russell's Theory of Descriptions. This theory, which is quite independent of the description theory of names, entails that a description like 'The author of these books' is not a referring expression at all, and so doesn't depend for its content on the existence of the author of these books (Aristotle).
3. For further discussion see Fitch 2004: 36–7.
4. I have altered the labelling for the sake of consistency.
5. For a similar but more detailed argument see Stanley 1997b.
6. To see this, consider the following contrived example. Let 'F' denote the following property: being a ruler of France in 1789 and being such that Aristotle doesn't exist. Then in the actual world there are no Fs; in a nearby world where Aristotle doesn't exist the F is Louis XVI. Now let 'G' be a property that applies to x if and only if $x = $ Aristotle or Fx. Then 'The G' is mildly but not persistently rigid: it denotes Aristotle at every world where he exists but Louis XVI at other worlds. Now 'The G' passes the intuitive test (p): the thing that is in fact the G (Aristotle) could not have both existed and failed to be the G.
7. Here we need the additional assumption that Aristotle is in fact the teacher of Alexander; but if this is false then (2) follows trivially.
8. Soames has argued as follows that 'Aristotle' is not synonymous with 'The actual teacher of Alexander':

   (i) At some possible world w Jones believes that Aristotle was a philosopher without believing of @ that the person who taught Alexander *there* was a philosopher (Premise)
   (ii) Necessarily Jones believes that the actual teacher of Alexander was a philosopher iff Jones believes, of @, that the person who taught Alexander there was a philosopher (Premise)
   (iii) If 'Aristotle' means the same as 'The actual teacher of Alexander' then necessarily, Jones believes that Aristotle was a philosopher if

Jones believes that the actual teacher of Alexander was a philosopher (Premise)

(iv) At some possible world w, Jones believes that Aristotle was a philosopher and Jones does not believe that the actual teacher of Alexander was a philosopher (from i, ii)

(v) 'Aristotle' does not mean the same as 'The actual teacher of Alexander' (from iii, iv)

The argument is valid: but the proponent of FRT need not accept premise (iii). We saw (arguments 2.1.3(iv) and 2.1.3(v)) that part of the motivation of FRT was that it explains the content of beliefs of the form 'Aristotle was F' in the context of certain metaphysical and epistemological constraints. And this means that the proponent of FRT must agree that 'Jones believes that Aristotle was F' has the same truth-value as (and is perhaps synonymous with) 'Jones believes that the actual teacher of Alexander was F'. But it doesn't follow that these sentences are *necessarily* equivalent (equally true or false of all counterfactual situations).

Waiving that objection, one might still raise a doubt about premise (ii). Soames' argument for (ii) is as follows (1998a:16)

(vi) 'The actual F was G' says of @ that the unique F there was G (Premise)

(vii) 'Jones believes that the actual F was G' is true of w iff at w Jones believes what 'The actual F was G' says (Premise)

(viii)'Jones believes that the actual F was G' is true at w iff at w Jones believes of @ that the unique F there was G (from vi, vii)

Premise (vi) is true but it is difficult to believe both that premise (vii) is true and that the argument is valid. To see this consider the following temporal analogue of it:

(ix) 'The present F is G' says of the present time that the unique F then is G (Premise)

(x) 'Jones believed that the present F is G' is true of time t iff at t Jones believed what 'The present F is G' says (Premise)

(xi) 'Jones believed that the present F is G' is true of time t iff at t Jones believed of the present time that the unique F then was G

Now (xi) is implausible. Suppose that we are describing the way things were in 1996. Then the sentence 'Mr Heath believed that the present Prime Minister is a Thatcherite' doesn't say that in 1996 Mr Heath believed of the present time (2006) that the Prime Minister *then* was a Thatcherite, which is the analogue of (xi): Mr Heath may have had no beliefs in 1996 about who would be PM in 2006. It says that Mr Heath believed in 1996 *of the present Prime Minister* (Mr Blair) that he was a Thatcherite. This is incompatible with (xi): hence either (x) is false or the argument is invalid. But then why can't we say the same about the argument from (vi) and (vii) to (viii)? If we are talking about *w*, then 'Jones believes that the actual *F* was *G*' says that Jones believes at *w*, *of the actual F*, that he is *G*; hence (viii) is false. So therefore is premise (ii). Nor can it be objected that Jones cannot have beliefs about the actual *F* at *w* because there he has no contact with the actual world. That may be true: but Jones *can* have contact with the actual *teacher of Alexander*: for from the mild rigidity of both 'Aristotle' and 'The actual teacher of Alexander' it follows that Aristotle could not have both existed and failed to be the actual teacher of Alexander: hence any world *w* at which Aristotle exists is a world where the actual teacher of Alexander exists.

9. Leaving aside such trivial conditions as the description 'the person identical with Gödel', which we know to be satisfied only by Gödel.

10. This was Russell's view (1956: 242–3).

11. Now it might sometimes happen that even *these* people do not have a description that actually picks out anyone: so something like the first premise of Kripke's semantic argument would apply to them. But in that case it is plausible that through sheer misfortune the name doesn't refer at all, in which case the relevant analogue of premise (4) would again be false.

12. The other objection was that the experts might themselves attribute the theory to Schmidt even though the layman doesn't. This possibility can be accommodated once we admit that the 'experts' to whom I defer will include not just experts about *logic* but other 'experts' about *Gödel*, e.g. his drinking companions, girl friends, etc. (or people who know these people). If all of *these* experts use the name 'Gödel' to refer to Schmidt then plausibly so do I.

13. For a discussion of this point and more examples see Jackson 1998: 209.

3 Necessity

1. See e.g. premises (20) and (21) at 2.2.5. These premises say that it is an essential property of *Aristotle* that he was Aristotle but an accidental property that he was the teacher of Alexander.

2. Hintikka 1999:130.

3. Della Rocca 2002 gives an argument that Kripke finds himself in the second case with respect to intuitions concerning the necessity of *identity* of individuals.

4. Lowe (2002: 104–6) considers a closely related argument and makes a different objection to the same step in it. For a recent attempt to derive the necessity of origin without relying on the sufficiency of origin see Rohrbaugh and deRosset 2004.

5. Hughes (2004:19–20) shows that this is a test for inflexibility.

6. There are some discrepancies between the NN and NN2 versions of this passage. I have quoted from the latter.

7. This includes the possibility that all the places that actually contain gold contain at *w* a substance that is like iron pyrites in that it resembles gold but unlike pyrites in that it has no actual instances. This stipulation is

needed if the argument is to have force against somebody who thinks that although gold might not have been identical to some actually existing compound, still it might have been identical to some compound that has no actual instances.

8. Kripke hints at these three possibilities at NN:310–11/NN2:109.

9. This argument is parallel to that endorsed by Kripke in opposition to the view that analyses of the form of (a) apply to *all* modal statements. He describes and opposes that view as follows: 'Thus if we say "Humphrey might have won the election (if only he had done such-and-such)", we are not talking about something that might have happened to *Humphrey* but to someone else, a "counterpart". Probably, however, Humphrey could not care less whether someone *else*, no matter how much resembling him, would have been victorious in another possible world' (NN:344n13/NN2:45n13). But if that is right then so is the following: when I say '*I* might have turned out to be a robot', I could not care less whether somebody *else*, no matter how similar his evidence, is a robot in another possible world.

10. There is a third possibility: you might be a materialist about sensational states but not propositional attitudes. For present purposes this position is in the same boat as (b).

11. This statement is an oversimplification. What we need (as we saw at 3.1.5) is that B is inflexible and A is mildly rigid. We can then establish that necessarily, if B exists then it is identical to A. And this is contrary to the fact (apparently supported by imaginative experiment) that Jones might have had B (the neural event) without A (the pain). This complication makes little difference to what follows: so I shall continue to use the loose formulation in the main text.

12. For (a) see Berkeley 1948–57 vol. 2:78 (*Principles* s87); for (b) see vol. 2:176 (First *Dialogue*).

13. This claim can be contested too: I think Wittgenstein *does* contest it (1967: section 258). But I do not fully understand Wittgenstein's argument so I won't pursue the matter.

4 Rule-Following

1. See also Blackburn 1984:28–9; McGinn 1984:91n21, 91n22.

2. See Wright (1980:37), Blackburn (1984:34–5), Goldfarb (1985:98), Zalabardo (1997 *passim*) and Kusch (2006:270n45). Millikan (1990:213n10) and Soames (1998b:338) both say that if Kripke did have something like this requirement then it is unclear why he doesn't immediately dismiss the dispositionalist account (see 4.3 below) as offtarget. But this is exactly what Kripke *does* say: W:23. Soames also says (1998b:341) that INR has little intuitive plausibility. I can only say that it seems to me to have a good deal of pre-theoretical plausibility.

3. See also W:21, 22, 24, 43 (the meaning fact *tells* me what to do) and 42 (it helps me *figure out* the answer).

4. Schopenhauer 1969 vol. 1: 99–100.

5. Berkeley 1948–57 vol. 1:92 (entry 756 in his *Commonplace Book*). See also vol. 1:74 (entry 599) and vol. 1:98 (entry 821).
6. Wright has objected that Kripke's argument against simplicity begs the question in favour of the sceptic because it assumes from the outset that there *are* no facts about what you meant (Wright 1984:108n6). It has been replied that Kripke is not *assuming* this but keeping a legitimately open mind about it (Miller and Wright 2002:10n16). This may be slightly unfair to Wright, whom I took in that passage only to be rejecting the idea that the finitude of your past uses of 'plus' by itself forecloses any *justification* of the hypothesis that you meant addition. But even if Wright is right about that it doesn't show that the simplicity response will cut any ice with the sceptic about meaning *facts*. It will not.
7. One argument against sensationalism that Kripke does not mention is Dummett's argument (1973) that private mental states cannot be ingredients of meaning because they cannot be manifested. Craig's response to this (1982) has always seemed to me decisive.
8. Note that if Kripke had held only the external and not the internal normativity requirement it would be difficult to make sense of this objection. The fact, if it is one, that we cannot have knowledge of the *sui generis* state in question, is grounds for denying that *sui generis* states satisfy INR. But it is no grounds for denying that they satisfy ENR.
9. See Hume 1949: I.iv.6; NN:355n77/NN2:155n77; W:121–2; Wright 1989a:148.
10. Or as it may be, what is postulated is not meaning addition by 'plus' but knowledge that '*x* plus *y*' denotes their sum: Davidson 2001a:109. Kripke himself says that the sceptical challenge may be interpreted as a question about what makes it true that you *denoted* addition by 'plus': W:10n8.
11. As Goldfarb is of course aware – 1985:98–9.

5 *Private Language*

1. I interpret this passage (the first full paragraph of W:67) as also attributing the *second* strategy to Hume when he is responding to his own scepticism about *causation*. He discusses inductive scepticism in the first three sentences of that paragraph and causal scepticism in the last two sentences of it.
2. Cf. Goldfarb 1985:100.
3. Wright (1984:104–5), Boghossian (1989:160), Wilson (1994:246), McDowell (1984:50–1) and Soames (1998b:318) may also take this view.
4. Exactly the same point applies to W:71–3, cited by Soames (1998b:318).
5. Byrne (1996), Kusch (2006:148–76).
6. Cf. Blackburn 1984:32–3.
7. See e.g. W:69, 70–1, 77, 86, 88, 89, 97 and 108.
8. Given the second distinction the present interpretation can also make as good sense as Byrne's of Kripke's remark that Wittgenstein may think

of meaning-facts as *sui generis* (W:51). It amounts to saying that meaning is factual in the minimal but not the robust sense.

9. It has been argued that Kripke might have held one of these positions (global non-factualism or factualism) on the grounds that their disjunction is in fact *true*: local non-factualism implies global non-factualism (Boghossian 1989:160). The clearest presentation of the arguments for this claim is in Kusch's recent book (2006:154–8). There he endorses three arguments:

(A) Wright's argument (pp.154–5) that local non-factualism (or 'projectivism' as he calls it) leads to global projectivism

(B) A sophisticated argument (pp.155–6) that local projectivism leads to global projectivism about *sentences*

(C) The sophisticated argument (pp. 156–7) that local projectivism leads to global projectivism about *propositions*

(D) The argument runs as follows:

> One immediate difficulty is presented by the meaning-truth platitude. If the truth value of S is determined by its meaning and the state of the world in relevant respects, then non-factuality in one of the determinants can be expected to induce non-factuality in one of the outcomes. (A rough parallel: if among the determinants of whether it is worth while going to see a certain exhibition is how well-presented the leading exhibits are, then, if questions of good presentation are not considered to be entirely factual, neither is the matter of whether it is worthwhile going to see the exhibition.) A projectivist view of meaning is thus, it appears, going to enjoin a projectivist view of what it is for a statement to be true. Whence, unless it is, mysteriously, possible for a projective statement to sustain a biconditional with a genuinely factual statement, the disquotational schema ' "p" is true iff p' will churn out the result that *all* statements are projective. (Wright 1984:104)

But I don't see why it *is* mysterious. As simple a biconditional as 'It is wrong to use cluster bombs in a war iff they harm civilians' appears to be 'sustainable' even if you are a projectivist abut the left-hand side and non-projectivist about the right (as most people probably are).

More generally: any local projectivist will have to distinguish between the kind of truth (minimal truth) that is appropriate for statements about which he is projectivist and the kind of truth (robust truth, factuality or whatever) that he thinks is appropriate for statements about which he is *not* a projectivist. So, why can the local projectivist not argue that such biconditionals (with a projective statement on the left and a factual statement on the right) are true (or acceptable) just in case both sides or neither meet whatever standard of truth (minimal or robust) is appropriate for *them*? In particular we can say that 'p' is factual but maintain that ' "p" is true iff p' is correct because the left-hand side is minimally true when and only when the right-hand side is robustly true (it corresponds to the facts). In that case we have not shown that local projectivism leads to global projectivism (cf. Hale 1997:379).

(B) My trouble with argument (B) derives from the distinction just mentioned between robust and minimal truth. Kusch argues as follows:

(ii) (φ) $(\sim\!\Delta$ $(\Delta$ (s, p), $\varphi))$
(iii) $\sim\!T$ $(\Delta$ (s, p))
(iv) $\sim\!\Delta$ (s, p)

Here lower-case roman letters are variables ranging over sentences and lower-case Greek letters are variables ranging over propositions. Δ (s, p) says that p expresses the truth-condition of s; Δ (s, φ) says that φ *is* the truth-condition of s. 'T' is the truth-predicate. The step from (ii) to (iii) relies on the principle P and the step from (iii) to (iv) relies on the principle Q.

(P) $T(x) \supset \exists\varphi$ $(\Delta$ (x, $\varphi))$
(Q) $\sim\!T(x) \supset \sim\!x$

But what does 'T' mean? Does it mean minimal truth (the sort that the projectivist grants to some statements of the form Δ (s, φ)) or does it mean robust truth (the sort that the global projectivist withholds from them all)?

If it means minimal truth then the (local) meaning-projectivist will reject the step from (ii) to (iii) because he will reject principle (P). He thinks that a statement like Δ (s, p) might be *minimally* true even though it purports to correspond to nothing in reality (and hence has no truth-conditions).

If it means robust truth then the local meaning-projectivist will reject the step from (iii) to (iv) because he will reject principle (Q). He thinks that even if a statement corresponds to no fact it might not follow that you can infer its negation: and it *will* not follow if the statement is an ascription of meaning, i.e. one about which he is himself projectivist. So in either case the argument is invalid and we have not shown that global projectivism follows from local projectivism about meaning.

(C) Essentially the same complaint applies to this argument. It tacitly relies on the step from (ii) to (iii) and also on the step from (viii) to (ix):

(viii) $\sim\!T$ $(\Delta$ (s, $\varphi))$
(ix) $\sim\!\Delta$ (s, $\varphi)$

But if 'T' is minimal truth then the local minimalist about meaning will reject the former step (from (ii) to (iii)) and if 'T' is robust truth then he will reject the latter step (from (viii) to (ix)). And this is for the same reasons as in (B). So again the argument doesn't show that local minimalism leads to global minimalism about meaning.

REFERENCES

Ayers, M. (1993), *Locke: Epistemology and Ontology*. 2 vols. London: Routledge.

Baker, G. and Hacker, P. (1984), *Scepticism, Rules and Language*. Oxford: Blackwell.

Bealer, G. (2002), 'Modal epistemology and the rationalist renaissance'. In Gendler and Hawthorne, 2002, 71–125.

Berkeley, G. (1948–57), *The works of George Berkeley, Bishop of Cloyne*. 9 vols. Edited by A. A. Luce and T. E. Jessop. London: Thomas Nelson.

Blackburn, S. W. (1984), 'The individual strikes back'. *Synthese*, 58, 325–63 (reprinted in Miller and Wright, 2002).

Block, N., ed. (1980), *Readings in the Philosophy of Psychology*. 2 vols. London: Methuen.

Boghossian, P. (1989), 'The rule-following considerations'. *Mind*, 98, 507–49 (reprinted in Miller and Wright, 2002).

Boyd, R. (1980), 'Materialism without reductionism: what physicalism does not entail'. In Block, 1980, vol. 1, 67–106.

Burge, T. (1988), 'Individualism and self-knowledge'. *Journal of Philosophy* 85 (11), 649–63.

Byrne, A. (1996), 'On misinterpreting Kripke's Wittgenstein'. *Philosophy and Phenomenological Research*, 56 (2), 339–43.

Chalmers, D. (1996), *The Conscious Mind*. Oxford: Oxford University Press.

Coates, P. (1986), 'Kripke's sceptical paradox: normativeness and meaning'. *Mind*, 95, 77–80.

—— (1997), 'Meaning, Mistake and Miscalculation'. *Minds and Machines*, 7, 171–97. Available at http://www.herts.ac.uk/philosophy/MMM.html

Craig, E. J. (1982), 'Meaning, use and privacy'. *Mind*, 91, 541–64.

Davidson, D. (1970), 'Mental Events'. In L. Foster and J. Swanson (eds), *Experience and Theory* (London: Duckworth), 79–101. Reprinted in Davidson, 2001b.

—— (2001a), 'The second person'. In his *Subjective, Intersubjective, Objective*, 107–22. Oxford: Oxford University Press.

—— (2001b), *Essays on Actions and Events*. Oxford: Oxford University Press.

Della Rocca, M. (2002), 'Essentialism vs. essentialism'. In Gendler and Hawthorne, 2002, 223–52.

Descartes, R. (1984–91), *Philosophical Writings of Descartes*. Translated by J. Cottingham, D. Murdoch and R. Stoothoff. Cambridge: Cambridge University Press.

Donnellan, K. (1983), 'Kripke and Putnam on natural kind terms'. In C. Ginet and S. Shoemaker (eds), *Knowledge and Mind* (Oxford: Oxford University Press), 84–104.

Dummett, M. A. E. (1963), 'The philosophical significance of Gödel's theorem'. *Ratio*, 5, 140–55 (reprinted in Dummett, 1978).

—— (1973), 'The philosophical basis of intuitionistic logic'. In H. E. Rose and J. C. Sheperdson (eds), *Logic Colloquium 1973* (North Holland), 5–40 (reprinted in Dummett, 1978).

—— (1978), *Truth and Other Enigmas*. London: Duckworth.

—— (1981a), *Frege: Philosophy of Language* (second edition). London: Duckworth.

—— (1981b), *The Interpretation of Frege's Philosophy*. London: Duckworth.

Evans, G. (1973), 'The causal theory of names'. *Aristotelian Society Supplementary Volume*, XLVII, 187–208.

Feldman, F. (1974), 'Kripke and the identity theory'. *Journal of Philosophy*, 71 (18), 665–76.

Fitch, G. W. (2004), *Saul Kripke*. Montreal: McGill-Queen's University Press.

Fodor, J. (1975), *The Language of Thought*. New York: Crowell (excerpted in Block, 1980).

—— (1990), *A Theory of Content and Other Essays*. Cambridge, Mass.: MIT Press.

—— (1998), *Concepts: Where Cognitive Science went Wrong*. Oxford: Oxford University Press.

Fogelin, R. (1987), *Wittgenstein* (second edition). London: Routledge.

Forbes, G. (1981), 'An anti-essentialist note on substances'. *Analysis*, 41, 32–7.

Frege, G. (1956), 'The thought: a logical inquiry'. *Mind*, 65, 289–311.

—— (1960), 'On sense and reference'. In P. Geach and M. Black (eds), *Translations from the Philosophical Writings of Gottlob Frege* (Oxford: Blackwell), 56–78.

Gendler, T. and Hawthorne, J., eds (2002), *Conceivability and Possibility*. Oxford: Oxford University Press.

Goldfarb, W. (1985), 'Kripke on Wittgenstein on rules'. *Journal of Philosophy*, 82 (9), 471–88 (reprinted in Miller and Wright, 2002).

Gomez-Torrente, M. (2006), 'Rigidity and essentiality'. *Mind*, 115, 227–59.

Hale, R. (1997), 'Rule-following, objectivity and meaning'. In Hale and Wright, 1997, 369–96.

—— and Wright, C., eds (1997), *A Companion to the Philosophy of Language*. Oxford: Blackwell.

Hanna, R. (1998), 'A Kantian critique of scientific essentialism'. *Philosophy and Phenomenological Research*, 58 (3), 497–528.

Hintikka, J. (1999), 'The emperor's new intuitions'. *Journal of Philosophy*, 96 (3), 127–47.

Horwich, P. (1995), 'Meaning, use and truth …'. *Mind*, 104, 355–68.

Hughes, C. (2004), *Kripke: Names, Necessity and Identity*. Oxford: Clarendon Press.

Hume, D. (1949), *A Treatise of Human Nature*. Edited with an analytical index by L. A. Selby-Bigge. Oxford: Clarendon Press.

Jackson, F. (1998), 'Reference and description revisited'. *Philosophical Perspectives*, 12, 201–18.

Kant, I. (1929), *Critique of Pure Reason*. Translated by Norman Kemp Smith. London: Macmillan.

Kroon, F. (1989), 'Circles and fixed points in description theories of reference'. *Nous*, 23, 373–82.

Kusch, M. (2006), *A Sceptical Guide to Meaning and Rules*. Chesham: Acumen.

Lewis, D. (1979), 'Scorekeeping in a language game'. *Journal of Philosophical Logic*, 8, 339–59 (reprinted in Lewis, 1980b).

—— (1980a), 'Mad pain and Martian pain'. In Block 1980, vol. 1, 216–22.

—— (1980b), *Philosophical Papers*. 2 vols. Oxford: Oxford University Press.

Loar, B. (1999), 'David Chalmers's *The Conscious Mind*'. *Philosophy and Phenomenological Research*, 59 (2), 465–72.

Locke, J. (1979), *Essay Concerning Human Understanding*. Edited by P. H. Nidditch. Oxford: Clarendon Press.

Lowe, E. J. (2002), *A Survey of Metaphysics*. Oxford: Oxford University Press.

Mackie, J. (1974), '*De* what *re* is *de re* modality?' *Journal of Philosophy*, 71 (16), 551–61.

McDowell, J. (1977), 'On the sense and reference of a proper name'. *Mind*, 86, 159–85 (reprinted in Moore, 1993).

—— (1984), 'Wittgenstein on following a rule'. *Synthese*, 58, 325–63 (reprinted in Miller and Wright 2002).

McGinn, C. (1977), 'Anomalous monism and Kripke's Cartesian intuitions'. *Analysis*, 37, 78–80.

—— (1984), *Wittgenstein on Meaning: An Interpretation and Evaluation*. Oxford: Blackwell (excerpted in Miller and Wright, 2002).

Mellor, D. H. (1977), 'Natural kinds'. *British Journal for the Philosophy of Science*, 28, 299–312.

Miller, A. (2000), 'Horwich, meaning and Kripke's Wittgenstein'. *Philosophical Quarterly*, 50 (199), 161–74.

—— and Wright, C., eds (2002), *Rule-Following and Meaning*. Chesham: Acumen.

Millikan, R. G. (1990), 'Truth rules, hoverflies and the Kripke-Wittgenstein paradox'. *Philosophical Review*, 99 (3), 323–53 (reprinted in Miller and Wright, 2002).

Moore, A. W., ed. (1993), *Meaning and Reference*. Oxford: Oxford University Press.

Quine, W.V.O. (1951), 'Two dogmas of empiricism'. *Philosophical Review*, 60, 20–43 (reprinted in Quine 1980).

—— (1960), *Word and Object*. Cambridge, Mass.: MIT Press.

—— (1976), 'Vagaries of definition'. In his *Ways of Paradox* (Cambridge, Mass.: Harvard University Press), 50–5.

—— (1980), *From a Logical Point of View* (second edn). Cambridge, Mass.: Harvard University Press.

Recanati, F. (1997), *Direct Reference*. Oxford: Blackwell.

Rohrbaugh, G. and deRosset, L. (2004), 'A new route to the necessity of origin'. *Mind*, 133, 705–25.

Russell, B. (1919), *Introduction to Mathematical Philosophy*. London: George Allen and Unwin.

—— (1956), 'The philosophy of logical atomism'. In G. Marsh (ed.), *Logic and Knowledge* (London: George Allen and Unwin), 177–281.

—— (1959), *The Problems of Philosophy*. Oxford: Oxford University Press.

Salmon, N. (1982), *Reference and Essence*. Oxford: Blackwell.

Schopenhauer, A. (1969), *The World as Will and Representation*. 2 vols. Trans. E. J. Payne. New York: Dover.

Soames, S. (1998a), 'The modal argument: wide scope and rigidified descriptions'. *Nous*, 32, 1–22.

—— (1998b), 'Facts, truth conditions and the skeptical solution to the rule-following paradox'. *Philosophical Perspectives*, 12, 313–48.

—— (2002), *Beyond Rigidity: The Unfinished Semantic Agenda of Naming and Necessity*. New York: Oxford University Press.

Stanley, J. (1997a), 'Names and rigid designation'. In Hale and Wright, 1997, 555–85.

—— (1997b), 'Rigidity and content'. In R. Heck (ed.), *Language, Thought and Logic: Essays in Honour of Michael Dummett* (Oxford: Oxford University Press), 131–56.

Tait, W. W. (1986), 'Wittgenstein and the "skeptical paradoxes"'. *Journal of Philosophy*, 83 (9), 475–88.

Williams, B. A. O. (1966), 'Imagination and the Self'. *Proceedings of the British Academy*, 52, 105–24 (reprinted in Williams, 1973).

—— (1973), *Problems of the Self*. Cambridge: Cambridge University Press.

Wilson, G. (1994), 'Kripke on Wittgenstein on Normativity'. *Midwest Studies in Philosophy*, 19, 366–90 (reprinted in Miller and Wright, 2002).

Wittgenstein, L. (1963), *Tractatus Logico-Philosophicus*. Translated by D. F. Pears and B. F. McGuinness. London: Routledge.

—— (1967), *Philosophical Investigations* (third edn). Translated by G. E. M. Anscombe. Oxford: Blackwell.

—— (1978), *Remarks on the Foundations of Mathematics* (third edn). Translated by G. E. M. Anscombe. Oxford: Blackwell.

Wright, C. (1980), *Wittgenstein on the Foundations of Mathematics*. London: Duckworth.

—— (1984), 'Kripke's account of the argument against private language'. *Journal of Philosophy*, 81(12), 759–78 (reprinted in Wright, 2001).

—— (1989a), 'Critical notice of *Wittgenstein on Meaning*'. *Mind*, 98, 289–305 (excerpted in Wright, 2001).

—— (1989b), 'Wittgenstein's Rule-Following Considerations and the Central Project of Theoretical Linguistics', in A. George, ed., *Reflections on Chomsky*, 246–54. Oxford: Blackwell (reprinted in Wright, 2001).

—— (1992), *Truth and Objectivity*. Cambridge, Mass.: Harvard University Press.

—— (2001), *Rails to Infinity*. Cambridge, Mass.: Harvard University Press.

—— (2002), 'The conceivability of naturalism'. In Gendler and Hawthorne, 2002, 401–39.

Zalabardo, J. L. (1997), 'Kripke's normativity argument'. *Canadian Journal of Philosophy*, 27 (4), 467–88 (reprinted in Miller and Wright, 2002).

—— (2003), 'Wittgenstein on accord'. *Pacific Philosophical Quarterly*, 84, 311–29.

INDEX